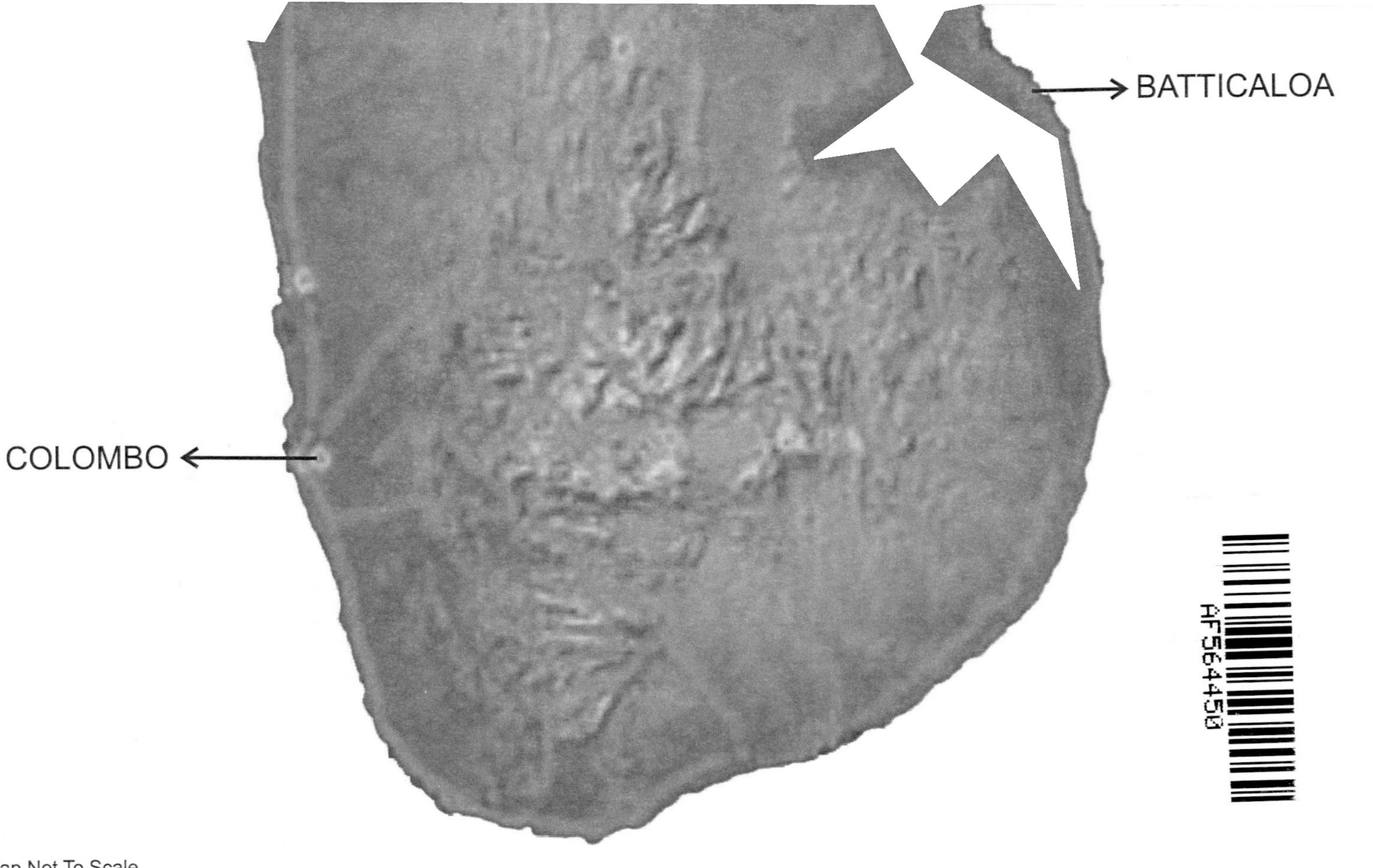

Map Not To Scale.

SRI LANKA

SRI LANKA

From War to Peace

Nitin A. Gokhale

Reprint, 2024

Published by Ashok Gosain and Ashish Gosain for
HAR-ANAND PUBLICATIONS PVT LTD
E-49/3, Okhla Industrial Area, Phase-II, New Delhi-110020
Tel: 41603490
E-mail: info@haranandbooks.com/haranand@rediffmail.com
Shop online at: www.haranandbooks.com

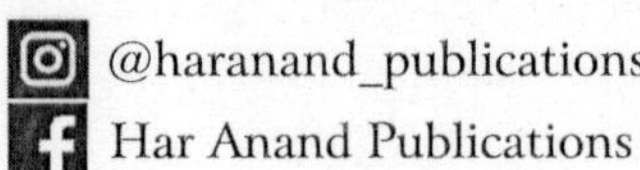
@haranand_publications
Har Anand Publications

Printed in India

Preface

The idea of writing this book popped into my mind on a short flight from Indore to Delhi. I was flying back after a talk on Military-Media relations at the prestigious Army War College in Mhow.

That morning the military audience had bombarded me with a barrage of questions about the recently concluded war in Sri Lanka since they knew I had just returned after reporting the conflict which had evoked worldwide interest.

As I shared my experience with Indian Army officers, it dawned on me that several aspects of Eelam War IV, as the conflict in the island nation came to be known, were largely unknown. Many were curious about the Sri Lankan Army's "winning formula," if there was one. Others wanted to know how and where the LTTE went wrong.

A book detailing the planning and execution of a military campaign that eliminated the world's most dreaded terrorist outfit was therefore waiting to be written.

As I started working on the project, old friend Shubho Bhattacharya introduced me to Narendra Kumar of Har-Anand Publications, who immediately showed keen interest in the book.

From then on, it has been a race against time.

To be honest, the book does not pretend to be a scholarly analysis of the Sri Lankan conflict.

Instead, my focus has been on the politico-military strategy adopted by Sri Lankan President Mahinda Rajapaksa and his military commanders to defeat an outfit which looked unbeatable in the past.

I was of course fortunate to report from the frontline since 2006, thanks to my bosses at NDTV who sent me there in the first place.

Many people have contributed in the writing of this book. Some of my sources and friends—Sri Lankan and Indian—have requested anonymity because of the sensitive information that they shared with me. They will remain unnamed.

Others who can be named here are: P K Balachandran, veteran journalist, long-time Sri Lanka watcher who generously shared his insights, Sri Lanka's Defence Secretary Gotabaya Rajapaksa, Gen. Sarath Fonseka, High Commissioner Romesh Jayasinghe, Sri Lanka's Foreign Secretary Palitha Kohona, Suggeeshwara Gunaratna of the Sri Lankan High Commission in Delhi, Lakshman Hulugalle of the Media Centre for National Security, Brig. Udaya Nanayakkara of the Sri Lankan Army, my Sri Lankan journalist friends like Thushara and Upendra, Anand Padmanabhan of *Taj Samudra* and finally cameraperson colleagues like Dhanpal and Sukumar who helped me stay ahead of the competition in reporting the conflict.

At NDTV, I must thank Radhika and Prannoy Roy, Barkha Dutt and Sonia Singh for allowing me to take some time off to write this book. At home, my wife Neha and our two boys Harsh and Utkarsh put up with my frequent absences and chaotic schedule most cheerfully. They also help me keep my feet firmly on ground.

The book would not have been published so quickly but for the enthusiasm showed by my publisher Narendra Kumar and his team.

Many have helped me in piecing together the fascinating transformation of the Sri Lankan defence forces that this book attempts to chronicle. Any shortcoming is however purely my fault.

NITIN A. GOKHALE

Contents

Chapter 1

The Final Days

May 19, 2009

A grim Vinayagyanmoorthi Muralitharan looked down at the body, inspected the belt, the ID card and the pistol that belonged to his former boss.

Moments later, he confirmed to the world that Vellupillai Prabhakaran, the elusive head of the Liberation Tigers of Tamil Eelam (LTTE) was dead.

It was a poignant moment for Muralitharan, better known as 'Col' Karuna.

Prabhakaran's trusted bodyguard at one time, 'Col' Karuna had risen through the LTTE's ranks to become one of his most effective and trusted military commanders before deciding to break away from the outfit in 2004.

Now a minister in the Sri Lankan government, Muralitharan was flown in into the battle zone on a small, deserted patch of land in the north-east of Sri Lanka that day to bolster the government's claim that the LTTE chief, considered the most dangerous terrorist leader in the world had indeed been killed by the Sri Lankan Army troops.

It was a rather tame end to a firebrand leader who had created from scratch a guerilla force that boasted of a large army, a potent naval arm and a rudimentary air wing. For more than a decade, he had controlled one-third of the island nation's territory and tormented the Sri Lankan state for over a quarter century.

It was not an easy victory for the Sri Lankan Army though.

It had taken the Army 33 months of a sustained, bloody and bitter military offensive to corner and finally kill Prabhakaran in a mangrove.

The man who led that campaign, Sri Lanka's Army Commander, Gen. Sarath Fonseka told me in an interview two days after the LTTE leader was killed that Prabhakaran and his close associates did try a last-minute deception-cum-offensive strategy.

During the interview in his office, Fonseka described Prabhakaran's final hours: "On 18th (May) night and 19th morning, top LTTE leadership divided itself into three different groups. They attacked our forward defence line along the Nanthikadal lagoon and did manage to break through. But they had reckoned without our second and third tier defences. These three groups were led by Jeyam, Pottu Amman and Soosai. Prabhakaran and his closest bodyguards thought they had managed to escape but in reality all these LTTE fighters, around 250 of them had got trapped between our first and the second defence lines. After fierce fighting that night and the next morning, almost all the top leadership got killed in the area. We discovered Prabhakaran's body on 19th morning."

Gen. Fonseka's measured and pithy narrative, meant primarily for a television audience (I was reporting for NDTV, India's leading 24-hour news network), does not fully describe what happened on May 18 and 19.

I later pieced together the monumental events of those two days through a combination of sources.

As Fonseka said, the final battle took place in a narrow stretch of land opening to the Indian Ocean from the East and to the Nanthikadal lagoon from the West. There was an open beachhead on the East, a dusty scrubby land in the middle and a waterlogged stretch full of mangroves on the West.

The area actually has one main road access, the Highway A-35 [Paranthan-Mullaittivu] that runs along the northwest- southeast axis, slanting itself towards the lagoon bank. *(see map)*.

There were plenty of manmade and natural barriers to overcome before one could get to the lagoon though.

Troops had to cross two causeways, march on an open beach and overcome several earth bunds and bunkers constructed by the LTTE to defend the last patch of territory in its possession.

Gen. Fonseka had deployed three Army Divisions and one Task Force in the final siege of the LTTE leadership.

Major General Kamal Gunrathne was commanding the 53 division and was also in-charge of the Task Force 8 commanded by Colonel G.V. Ravipriya.

Brig Shavindra Silva's 58 Division which had played the main offensive role through the 33 months of Eelam War IV, continued to be the spearhead.

And then there was the 59 Division, headed by Major General Prasanna Silva, which was holding the main defensive line south of Vadduvakal causeway even as the other two divisions launched the offensive from the north. With such a massive deployment, the LTTE leadership, including Prabhakaran was truly boxed in.

There was only one possible escape route for Prabhakaran and that was through the lagoon. The Sri Lankan Army was aware of this possibility and had deployed its troops accordingly.

The countdown to the final battle actually began on May 17.

According to officers involved in the operations, the LTTE made its first attempt to escape that morning. Over 150 cadres, under the leadership of a senior leader Jeyam launched a surface attack across the lagoon using small boats around 3 a.m. and managed to land on the western bank just short of the army's defence line at Keppularu.

Troops of the 5 Vijayaba Infantry Regiment and 19 Sri Lanka Light Infantry were waiting in anticipation. After a fierce, three-hour long battle on the western bank of the lagoon, 148 LTTE cadres died. The Army too suffered several casualties.

But the Tamil Tigers had failed to breach the defence line and open an escape route for Prabhakaran and other top leaders. It was clear through this attack that the Tigers were trying to establish a foothold on the banks of the lagoon and then open up an escape route for Prabhakaran into the Muthiyankaddu jungle.

Gen. Fonseka told me: "We knew that the LTTE would try this option first. If they had managed to establish a foothold there, the leaders would have escaped across the lagoon and disappeared into the huge Muthiyankaddu jungle, making our task of finding them that much more difficult. But we had anticipated their move since their tactics had not changed over the years."

Even as this skirmish ended, the last group of civilians, held hostage by the LTTE walked into the government controlled area. Now the army was free to deal with well-trained and well-armed hardcore LTTE cadres.

In Colombo, Gen. Fonseka was personally monitoring the situation.

On ground, his formation commanders had drawn up an elaborate plan to trap Prabhakaran.

The world's media was meanwhile descending on Colombo in droves, in anticipation of the LTTE's military defeat and the possible capture or elimination of Prabhakaran.

I too flew into Colombo on May 16, the day when India was glued to its television sets, catching the latest results of the general elections.

For the next 24 hours, all of us were on the edge, tapping all possible sources for news from the frontline. But the official stand remained constant: Top LTTE leaders are cornered in a small patch of land, but beyond that there was no other information.

As night fell on May 17, the Sri Lankan army braced for further attacks by the remaining LTTE fighters.

And sure enough, the first desperate charge by the Tamil Tigers came after midnight on May 17.

The defence ministry website, defence.lk quotes Lieutenant Colonel Keerthi Kottachchi, Commanding Officer of the 17 Gemunu Watch regiment as saying that this attack came in the form of a deception.

According to him, a group of terrorists disguised as civilians asked the troops manning the defences along the lagoon bank to let them in around 2.30 a.m. on May 18.

"It was my troops that manned the civilian rescue point at Karayamullivaikkal. The terrorists had come along the lagoon bank and were hiding in a small islet in front of our defences. Only a small group came to our line and pleaded with the officer there to let them in saying several injured people were among the group," Colonel Kottachchi was quoted as saying.

However, Colonel Kottachchi was well briefed by his Task Force Commander, Colonel G.V. Ravipriya and Brigade Commander, Lieutenant Colonel Lalantha Gamage on the possibility that LTTE cadres might launch an attack disguising themselves as civilians.

"Since all civilians were already rescued, I had given strict instruction to not to take anyone in until dawn. Around 3 a.m., the officer at the rescue point reported that the group which described itself as civilians was becoming violent and trying to breach the defence line. So, I ordered him to fire two shots into the air to control the situation," he said.

"Suddenly nearly 200 terrorists opened up fire and charged into our positions," the Colonel said.

The end battle had been truly joined.

Describing the operation, Lieutenant Colonel Lalantha Gamage, the 681 Brigade Commander said: "The terrorists managed to neutralize two of our bunkers, opening about a 100 metre gap in the defences. But after the first charge, most of the initial intruders stepped into firing range of our machine guns and died on the lagoon bank itself. The commandos and infantrymen killed about 100 LTTE cadres including some of the most senior leaders even before they stepped out of the water," he added.

Meanwhile, another group comprising over 100 LTTE cadres tried to breach 58 Division defence, north of Vadduvakkal, at first light. This group also met the same fate at the hands of Special Forces soldiers and infantrymen.

A large majority of the other LTTE cadres who managed to swim across the lagoon to step on the ground were killed by the 58 Division troops manning the defence line on the coastal side of the A-35 road. Over 100 other LTTE cadres who remained hiding in the mangroves were killed by the commandos, Special Forces and infantry troops conducting mopping up operations.

The first group to meet its end at the hands of army's counter penetration troops was in fact led by Prabhakaran's elder son, Charles

Anthony. The group was gunned down before they could walk the 250m distance from the point of infiltration.

Charles Anthony's battered body was discovered and identified almost immediately.

It was May 18.

As we flashed the news and analyzed the implications from far away Colombo, rumors, half-truths and lies were swirling endlessly.

Several conflicting reports about Prabhakaran's whereabouts led to confused reporting all across the media that day.

One report said he had managed to escape into the Muthiyankaddu jungle; another quoted senior military officials as saying Prabhakaran, Sea Tigers Chief Soosai and LTTE's intelligence Chief Pottu Amman were gunned down while trying to escape in a hijacked ambulance, their bodies burnt beyond recognition after the vehicle caught fire.

As it turned out, none of these reports was true.

A senior military official clarified later: "It was an ambulance that belonged to the Advanced Dressing Station of the Air mobile brigade. It was destroyed by the terrorists may be in a failed attempt to hijack the vehicle. We initially received reports from the soldiers that there was a burnt body lying close to the destroyed vehicle. The body had a structure resembling Prabhakaran. But that information was proven wrong," he added.

The clarification came much later. For most of May 18, we in the media kept reporting and repeating the story even when the defence ministry and the army refrained from officially confirming the reports of Prabhakaran's death.

On the battlefield itself, troops had beaten back every desperate attempt by the LTTE leadership to escape the dragnet. Through the day, mopping up operations continued across the battle zone. Over 350 bodies of LTTE cadres were recovered. But it was a major task to identify each of those slain cadres. Intelligence officials got down to work, comparing photographs available with them with each of the dead.

It was a painstaking job. But by late evening that day, the Army had been able to positively identify more than 30 top- and middle-level Tamil Tigers.

There was however no sign yet of Prabhakaran, Soosai or Pottu Amman.

So there was no let up in the watch.

Field Commanders, acutely conscious of the possibility that Prabhakaran and his top associates may still be hiding in the area, did not allow the troops to relax. The next 12 hours were going to be crucial.

And May 19, 2009 indeed turned out to be a big day for Sri Lanka.

At 9.30 a.m. President Mahinda Rajapaksa began his address to the Parliament. He surprised everyone by beginning his speech in Tamil. But Rajapaksa too was silent on Prabhakaran's whereabouts, raising doubts whether the Army had actually finished the war.

But unknown to many of us, the quarter-century old civil war in Sri Lanka had already reached it climax early that morning after a dramatic fight in a deserted mangrove.

Throughout the night of May 18 and the early hours of May 19, Major General Kamal Gunarathne, Colonel G.V. Ravipriya and Lieutenant Colonel Lalantha Gamage were planning the final assault on the last remaining patch of mangroves that lies south of the causeway at Karayamullavaikkal.

The commandos had already cleared a large part of the mangroves on the previous day. At 8.30 a.m. the second clearing operation was launched in the remaining part of the mangroves by both commandos and 4 VIR troops.

Lieutenant Colonel Lalantha Gamage, and Lieutenant Colonel Rohitha Aluwihare, Commanding Officer of the 4 VIR were personally leading the assault.

Two 8-man teams and one 4-man team of 4 VIR Bravo company were scouring the mangroves.

As soon as the first team lead by Sergeant SP Wijesinghe entered the mangroves, they came under heavy small arms fire. The soldiers had to take cover behind thorny bushes in chest deep water. After an hour of intense exchange of fire, Wijesinghe's team advanced some 50 metres and found five bodies. All the slain LTTE cadres were carrying pistols and revolvers.

Wijesinghe and team instantly knew they were onto the big fish since only bodyguards of top leaders in the LTTE were allowed to carry pistols.

The veteran Sergeant immediately alerted his Brigade Commander and the Commanding Officer.

Moments later, one of the bodies was identified as that of Vinodan, one of the most senior bodyguards of the inner protection team of the LTTE leader. "Within seconds we knew the importance of the finding," Lieutenant Colonel Lalantha Gamage later said.

The troops were now too close to their ultimate target to take any chances. Major General Kamal Gunaratne, who was closely following every move of the assault team, ordered Sgt. Wijesinghe and his team to form a defensive line and plug any possible escape route. Another eight man infantry team and a four man commando force was sent as reinforcement from the flank to support Sgt. Wijesinghe's advance party.

The second team was lead by Sergeant TM Muthubanda.

As soon as these teams advanced, they were fired upon. Another intense gun battle ensued. After an hour of heavy exchange of fire, the mangroves suddenly went silent. The two team leaders cautiously advanced into the bushes to find 18 bodies scattered around.

Among them was Vellupillai Prabhakaran, the man who had tormented the Sri Lankan state for over 30 years.

It was 8.30 a.m. on May 19, 2009.

The Army commander was immediately informed.

But Gen. Fonseka wanted to be doubly sure before announcing the news to the world.

After consultations with Defence Secratary Gotabaya Rajapaksa, it was decided to request Vinagyanmoorty Muralitharan alias 'Col' Karuna to positively identify the slain LTTE leader's body.

Daya Master, who had surrendered to the authorities less than a month ago after being an important link between the LTTE and the media, was also flown in into the battlefield.

Both immediately confirmed that the body lying on the banks of the Nanthikadal Lagoon was indeed that of Prabhakaran—the man who created and led the world's most dreaded terrorist outfit.

The military defeat of the LTTE was complete. The President, who had just finished his address to the Parliament, was informed.

An hour later, images of Prabhakaran's body, dressed in military fatigues, were flashed on television screens across the globe.

There was total disbelief. And several unanswered questions.

How could a man who introduced so many innovative terrorist methods die such an inglorious death? Did he not have an escape plan? Why didn't he consume cyanide as many of his cadres did when cornered? Why didn't the man, who always had a surprise move up his sleeve, no matter how adverse the circumstances, manage to turn the tables this time?

Only his closest aides or family would have been able to provide correct answers but all of them are now dead.

Several days after Prabhakaran's death was announced, there were many whispers about how the Army had captured Prabhakaran and his family alive, kept them in custody, tortured them and then executed them all in cold blood.

Another version said Prabhakaran himself shot the entire family—wife Madhivadhani Erambu, daughter Duvaraga (23) and younger son Balachandran (11)—before killing himself, after they were surrounded by the army.

But none of the rumors are verifiable, although it must be said that the government is silent on Madhivadhani, Duvaraga and Balachandran's fate, leaving a lot of scope for speculation.

In the week after his death many pro-LTTE websites, Tamil magazines and newspapers had gone to the extent of claiming that Prabhakaran was still alive and the body that was displayed by the Sri Lankan army as the LTTE chief's was in fact that of a look alike! But the Sri Lankan government had no doubt that its army had finally eliminated Prabhakaran. Nearly a month later, a DNA test also confirmed that the body recovered from the banks of the Nanthikadal lagoon was of the LTTE supremo.

So what led to Prabhakaran's ultimate downfall?

Several factors contributed to the LTTE's military defeat.

But 'Col' Karuna's remark to me, a day after he identified Prabhakaran's body, perhaps encapsulates in one sentence, the reason for Prabhakaran's self-destruction.

Karuna, who admitted feeling a bit sad to see his former boss meeting such a violent end, said: "Prabhakaran was not a man of peace. He only knew how to destroy, not build."

There cannot be a more accurate assessment of the man who gave the world the cult of suicide bombers. Prabhakaran was the man who ordered assassination of Presidents and Prime Ministers. He was the man who inspired and motivated thousands of young men and women to sacrifice their lives for the cause of Tamil Eelam.

He however did not know when to quit.

Over the years, a succession of victories had made the LTTE chief complacent and overconfident of his own abilities which prevented him from accepting changed realities. Prabhakaran lived and died as a terrorist without graduating into a political leader.

'Col' Karuna says Prabhakaran himself sowed the seeds of his own destruction in the post-2002 era when he accepted a Norway-brokered ceasefire but failed to carry forward the process.

CHAPTER 2

Beginning of the End

A REVOLT AND A FAILED ASSASSINATION

By January 2000, Prabhakaran was the lord and master of everything that he surveyed in Sri Lanka's north and north-east, a region collectively known as Wanni.

His writ ran over the entire districts of Mullaitivvu, Killinochchi and parts of Vavuniya. Even in the Eastern province, the LTTE had control over Batticaloa and parts of Trincomalee.

Prabhakaran had established administrative control over approximately 16,000 sq km of Sri Lanka's total area of 65,000 sq km.

He had a full-fledged army, a powerful naval wing and he was in the process of setting up a rudimentary air wing.

The LTTE had its own police, a functioning judiciary, even a passport control office at the border that separated the Tamil Tiger-held areas from the government-controlled parts of Sri Lanka.

Perhaps Prabhakaran's only regret was that Jaffna, the ancient Tamil town, for long the heart of Tamil struggle in Sri Lanka, was not under the LTTE's control.

And yet at the turn of the century, Prabhakaran was ruling a de facto state, a nation within a nation.

Then 9/11 happened.

As Al Qaeda fanatics slammed their planes into the World Trade Centre in New York on September 11, 2001, international opinion on non-state organizations and their ideas of revolution changed forever.

The world now looked at these outfits as terrorists.

Aware of the new realities, Prabhakaran was forced to reassess his strategy in dealing with the Sri Lankan state.

In his customary annual address on November 27 that year, Prabhakaran asked the West to redefine its concept of terrorism to exclude groups like his own that, according to him, used violence for "a concrete political objective." Prabhakaran denied being a terrorist and said he represented a "people's movement."

"Western democratic nations should provide a clear and comprehensive definition of the concept of terrorism that would distinguish between freedom struggles based on the right to self-determination and blind terrorist acts based on fanaticism," he appealed.

The speech was posted on prominent Tamil websites. "We are fighting and sacrificing our lives for the love of a noble cause, that is, human freedom. We are freedom fighters," he said.

By then, the LTTE had been proscribed by India, the U.K., the U.S., besides Sri Lanka, and was recently included in a list of terrorist groups by Canada.

It was against this backdrop that Prabhakaran agreed to meet Norwegian mediators in December 2001 and showed openness to negotiate with Colombo.

By a strange coincidence Ranil Wickramasinghe of the United National Party (UNP), who had promised to initiate another peace process in Sri Lanka, swept to power and became Prime Minister.

A fortnight after Ranil Wickramasinghe took office Prabhakaran announced a month long ceasefire.

The government immediately reciprocated and said it was lifting the economic blockade of the LTTE-held territories.

Events moved rapidly thereafter.

In February 2002, the LTTE and the Government of Sri Lanka signed on an agreement formalizing the ceasefire. Norway was accepted by both sides as the main negotiator.

A Sri Lanka Monitoring Mission (SLMM) facilitated by Norway and other Nordic countries was set up.

By August that year, Colombo lifted the ban on the LTTE paving the way for direct talks between the two sides. From September 2002 onwards, several rounds of negotiations took place at Phuket in Thailand, in Norway and in Germany.

Peace was in the air.

But in Colombo's political establishment, signs of trouble were apparent.

For the first time in Sri Lanka's political history, the President and the Prime Minister were from different parties.

President Chandrika Kumaratunga belonged to the Sri Lanka Freedom Party (SLFP) while Wickramasinghe, the Prime Minister was from the opposing UNP. Their differences over a likely solution to the Tamil issue, were soon threatening to overtake the peace process.

President Kumaratunga's SLFP was opposed to the federal solution suggested by Prime Minister Wickramasinghe and his party, the UNP. Wickramasinghe, a pacifist, wanted to use the ceasefire to bring a permanent solution to the Tamil issue.

The negotiations were not going anywhere.

In less than a year after they began, the LTTE decided to suspend the talks saying they were not happy with some of the issues. But it did not altogether withdraw. Instead, the Tamil Tigers came up with their own proposal calling for an Interim Self-Governing Authority (ISGA). The ISGA, the LTTE said, would be controlled by them and have broad powers in the north and the east.

Predictably, the proposal provoked a strong protest in the Sinhala-dominated South. The majority community saw the ISGA proposal as a precursor to the division of the country. That perception cornered Prime Minister Wickramasinghe and eventually led to his downfall.

Playing to the Sinhala gallery, President Kumaratunga declared a state of emergency and took over three key government ministries from UNP in December 2003, undermining Wickramasinghe further.

As 2004 dawned, no one in Sri Lanka would have imagined how a couple of momentous events that took place over the next 24 months were to change the course of Sri Lanka's history and seal Prabhakaran's fate.

The first was the general elections in April 2004.

The elections were forced on the country after the rift between President Kumaratunga and Prime Minister Wickramasinghe reached breaking point. With elections round the corner, Kumaratunga allied herself with the ultra right wing JVP, opposed to any concessions to the LTTE.

The new alliance fought the April elections on a new platform called the UFPA and emerged victorious. That's when the second noteworthy event of 2004 took place.

Mahinda Rajapaksa was appointed Prime Minister of Sri Lanka.

A politician from Sri Lanka's deep South, Mahinda Rajapakse had cut his political teeth in the tough environs of Sri Lanka's local and provincial politics. Till the late 1990s he was counted among the second rung leaders of the SLFP. And was therefore somewhat of a surprise choice for the post of Prime Minister in the summer of 2004.

Barely a month before Rajapaksa was being sworn in as Prime Minister, another significant development of 2004 was unfolding.

For the first time, the LTTE was facing internal dissent, something which it had not witnessed in a decade.

And leading the rebellion was LTTE's Eastern Regional Commander Vinayagamoorthy Muralitharan alias 'Col' Karuna.

In March that year, Prabhakaran, after a token meeting of the LTTE's highest decision making body, announced the expulsion of 'Col' Karuna.

Prabhakaran accused him of treachery against the Tamil people "at the instigation of some malicious elements."

He immediately replaced Karuna by his unranked former deputy, Ramesh. Two other Eastern second rung leaders, Ram and Kousalyan, were appointed Deputy Commander and political head, respectively of Batticaloa-Amparai district in the East.

Yet, in a last ditch effort to avert split in the group, Prabhakaran offered Karuna an amnesty that would have allowed him to lead a private life.

This was unprecedented.

In the past, even a whiff of a rebellion was enough for Prabhakaran to imprison and kill anyone who went against him. In 1993, Prabhakaran had not spared his cousin Mahataya, after reports about Mahataya's dalliance with India's external spy agency Research and Analysis Wing or RAW had surfaced. Mahatayya and nearly 250 of his followers were put on mock trial and killed after being tortured mercilessly for months.

Karuna, aware of Prabhakaran's past actions, was careful not to fall into the trap of the amnesty offer. Moreover, unlike Mahattaya, Karuna commanded the loyalties of over 6,000 fighters in the East. He was an adept military commander and was master of his area. Even if he wanted to punish Karuna for his rebellion, Prabhakaran would have had to launch a full-fledged operation in the East which, under the circumstances, would have been difficult.

In 2004, LTTE was a party to a ceasefire brokered by international observers. Prabhakaran was at that point trying to change the LTTE's image to that of a democratic, tolerant organization which was compelled to take up arms and resort to terrorism in absence of any other alternative. Prabhakaran did not have an option but to reconcile with Karuna's defection.

But what prompted Karuna to rebel and break away?

In an interview to me in Colombo, Karuna, now a minister in the Rajapaksa government explained why he chose to part ways with Prabhakaran after 22 years in the LTTE.

> "*My problem with Prabhakaran was mainly because of his rigid attitude. For two years since 2002 after LTTE acceded to the Norway-brokered Ceasefire, I was in the delegation that held negotiations all over the globe. During our interaction and travels, we had realized that the world was no longer tolerant of violence, even if it was for a good cause.*
>
> *In 2004, after I returned from Geneva, I went up to Prabhakaran and showed him a draft agreement proposed by the negotiators. One glance at it and he tore the draft and threw it in my face accusing me of betraying the Tamil cause.*

His anger was over the proposal which talked about an autonomous arrangement for the Tamils within a united Sri Lanka. I kept quiet at that moment but later tried to reason with him.

I pointed out to him that the world is no longer tolerant of any violent activity and therefore no matter how many soldiers we kill and how many victories we earn, the LTTE would never be regarded as a liberation movement. We will always be branded as terrorists, no matter what we do, I told him.

But he would not listen. He wanted Eelam (separate homeland) or nothing.

When he asked me to send a contingent of 1000 soldiers to the North, I knew Prabhakaran was once was getting ready for war.

Then there was another problem within the LTTE.

Since Prabhakaran came from Jaffna, the leadership and all important posts within the organization were always given to the Northern Tamils. Although most of the fighters came from the East, we never got our due. When I raised these issues, Pottu Amman and Nadesan (LTTE's intelligence wing chief and Tigers police chief respectively) started poisoning Prabhakaran's mind against me. I realized that they would like to get rid of me much in the same fashion as Mahattaya. But I read the signs early and decided to break away."

Not keeping Karuna in his fold was to prove one of Prabhakaran's biggest mistakes.

By then Karuna was already an established military leader in the LTTE.

Through the mid-1990s, his importance to Prabakaran had grown in direct proportion to the escalation of the war in the North, especially after the Sri Lankan army had ousted the LTTE from the Jaffna peninsula in1996.

Since he no longer controlled the peninsula, Prabhakaran was robbed of a ready-made territorial base from which to draw his manpower. He looked to eastern Sri Lanka, where his cadres controlled entire villages. Karuna was his points man in those years.

Karuna had in fact come to the LTTE's rescue in th late 1990s when the Sri Lankan Army launched an operation to take control of a strategic highway in northern Sri Lanka. He led thousands of fighters from the East for the counter-offensive, successfully thwarting the advance, inflicting hundreds of casualties on the Sri Lankan armed forces on what came to be known as the Highway of Blood.

Karuna also led the LTTE's Unceasing Waves offensives through which the group regained all the territory it had lost to the Government in the northern Wanni mainland in 1999-2000. During that conflict, the LTTE too suffered heavy casualties, most of the killed cadres belonged to the East. Despite such a huge contribution, Tamils in Batticaloa and Trincomalee never got their due even within the LTTE. Karuna's rebellion gave vent to that frustration among the eastern cadres.

It was a bitter parting.

Karuna, had joined the group as a 19 year old, become Prabhakaran's bodyguard in the mid-Eighties, traveling with him to India and even undergoing training at camps run by RAW for the fledgling LTTE. Over the years, he had self-developed his military skills and ably led the LTTE's fighting formations to emerge as a top commander.

Karuna's departure was a big blow to the LTTE. Initially, Prabhakaran did try to patch up with Karuna but the eastern commander wanted that Prabhakaran should remove Pottu Amman and police chief Nadesan. Pottu Amman and Nadesan wanted to launch an investigation into what they called financial misappropriation by Karuna. When Prabhakaran refused to act against the duo, Karuna knew it was time to quit.

When the patch up bid failed, Prabhakaran sent out killer squads to secretly eliminate Karuna. But it wasn't easy to get at the former Eastern Commander. He had kept his army of supporters in tact. They were a formidable force. And he had opened a channel with RAW and the Sri Lankan government.

For two years, Prabhakaran tried to eliminate Karuna but he managed to evade the killers. For two years he stayed incognito in

India in places like Pune and Trivandrum, masquerading as a Malayasian businessman.

But he was to soon return.

If Karuna's departure was a big blow to the LTTE, Prabhakaran's decision to eliminate Lakshman Kadirgamar, a highly respected Tamil lawyer turned politician in August 2005 led to far-reaching consequences for the Tamil Tigers. Then Sri Lankan Foreign Minister, Kadrigamar had developed extensive contacts with international diplomatic community. Despite being a Tamil, he had been sharply critical of the LTTE.

On August 12, 2005, Kadirgamar was shot by an LTTE sniper in Colombo as he was getting out of the swimming pool at his private residence. Prabhakaran had him killed because he believed that Kadirgamar had been responsible for the LTTE being banned as a terrorist organization by a number of countries including the United States, Canada, India and the European Union.

Kadirgamar had on many occasions mentioned the LTTE's threats to his life.

Speaking to *The Hindu*, he said "The LTTE can get me anytime. I get very serious reports that things are hotting up."

There was widespread condemnation of the LTTE. India's Ministry of External Affairs called Kadirgamar's killing as a terrorist act.

Then UN Secretary General Kofi Annan said: "Sri Lanka has lost a deeply respected statesman dedicated to peace and national unity."

Then U.S. Secretary of State Condoleezza Rice, who had met Kadirgamar two months before his assassination, condemned the killing as a "senseless murder and vicious act of terror" and urged Sri Lankans not to let it lead to resumed civil war. She praised Kadirgamar as a man of "dignity, honor and integrity, who devoted his life to bringing peace to Sri Lanka."

Peace brokers Norway also condemned the assassination, with Foreign Minister Jan Petersen describing it as "an atrocious crime and a tragedy for Sri Lanka."

Prabhakaran may not have realized it then but Kadirgamar's assassination cost the LTTE dearly in the long run. That single act of killing, led to the marginalization of the LTTE from the international community. From that point, the LTTE lost all sympathy it enjoyed in the eyes of foreign nations.

Ironically, Prabhakaran made a bigger mistake in November that year by indirectly helping Mahinda Rajpakasa to win the Presidential election against Ranil Wickramasinghe.

As it happened, Prabhakaran ordered the Tamils in the North and the East to boycott the Presidential elections. Ranil Wickramasinghe, the architect of the 2002 Ceasefire Agreement with the LTTE, was hoping to get en masse backing of the Tamils but Prabhakaran's boycott call robbed him of that opportunity and allowed Rajapaksa to scrape through.

Apparently, the LTTE chief, assessed the strengths and weaknesses of the two Presidential candidates—Wickramasinghe and Rajapaksa—and calculated that Mahinda Rajpakasa would be much easier to manipulate since he was a relative newcomer to the high office. So he ordered the Tamils to stay away from the polls fully aware that the poll boycott would hurt Ranil Wickramasinghe.

But perhaps Prabhakaran should have read Rajapaksa's intentions a little more closely.

Launching his Presidential campaign on October 18, 2005, Mahinda Rajpaksa had visibly articulated his thoughts on the ethnic issue.

"I strongly believe in achieving peace without going to war," he said in his speech at the manifesto launching ceremony. He added that he would protect the country's unity, sovereignty and security and preserve the civil rights of all groups.

"I totally refuse the concept of traditional homelands. Sri Lanka is a traditional homeland for every Sri Lankan," he said.

Rajapaksa had clearly hinted that he was not in favor of giving any special treatment to the Tamils simply because they were in a majority in the North and the East.

Prabhakaran should have been able to read between the lines and understand how Rajapaksa intended to deal with the LTTE if he were elected President.

But the LTTE leader was losing his touch with the ground realities, isolated as he was from the world, sitting in the jungles of Wanni.

So in less than two years after he had become Prime Minister, Mahinda Rajapaksa ascended to the all-powerful seat of Sri Lanka's executive President.

It was a rise very few people were ready for.

Now he was chief executive and commander in chief of the armed forces.

Despite his hawkish image, Rajapaksa did make it clear that he was in favor of continuing the ceasefire and negotiations with the LTTE.

Prabhakaran also indirectly seemed to reciprocate the sentiment.

In his so-called annual speech, made on November 27, 2005 the LTTE chief conveyed the message that the LTTE was willing to give a reasonable time frame for President Rajapaksa to revive the faltering peace process.

But he also warmed that the Tigers would "renew their struggle" in 2006 if the government did not take serious moves toward peace.

Meanwhile, President Rajapaksa continued to show patience and even sent personal emissaries to talk to the LTTE leadership. Deep down however, the new President had made up his mind to finish the LTTE.

Of course no one outside his immediate circle knew of the President's intentions.

His first move in the grand plan to take on the LTTE militarily was to appoint Maj Gen. GSC Fonseka as Sri Lanka's 18th Army Commander.

It was a deliberate choice.

President Rajapaksa was preparing for war.

He could not have handpicked a better general.

An infantry soldier, commissioned in the Sinha regiment in 1970, Fonseka had spent the major part of his career fighting the LTTE and was still game for another fight.

A man of imposing physique, Fonseka is known to have an equally big heart and a sharp military intellect. Throughout his career, he had displayed raw courage and sterling leadership. Even before he took over, Fonseka's exploits at various stages in his career were legion in an army that had an image of a lethargic and laid back force.

During one of his daring exploits to rescue troops trapped in the Jaffna Fort Garrison, one of his closest friends was a man called Gotabaya Rajapaksa, then a lieutenant colonel.

Now 15 years later, destiny had brought the two men together again. Mahinda Rajapaksa had appointed his brother Gotabaya as the new Defence Secretary. Gotabaya had become a US citizen after leaving the army in the 1992 but was back to help the President. Together they were preparing for the coming war.

The President now wanted the Gotabaya-Fonseka duo to deliver Prabhakaran to him, dead or alive.

By January 2006, skirmishes between the army and the LTTE had escalated alarmingly although both sides had stopped just short of an actual war.

There was increased violence, including Claymore mine attacks which killed 150 government troops, clashes between the Sea Tigers and the Sri Lanka navy, and the killings of sympathizers on both sides including Taraki Sivaram, a journalist who ran the highly read Tamilnet.com website, and Joseph Pararajasingham, a pro-LTTE MP.

In light of this violence, the co-chairs of the Tokyo Donor conference called on both parties to return to the negotiating table. The co-chairs—the United States in particular—were heavily critical of the violence perpetrated by the LTTE. US State Department officials, as well as the US ambassador to Sri Lanka, gave warnings to the Tigers claiming a return to hostilities would mean that the Tigers would face a "more capable and more determined" Sri Lankan military.

In a last-minute effort to salvage an agreement between the parties, Norwegian special envoy Erik Solheim and the LTTE theoretician Anton Balasingham arrived on the island. The parties severely disagreed on the location of the talks; however, continued efforts produced a breakthrough when both parties agreed on February 7, 2006, that new talks could be held in Geneva on February 22 and February 23. These talks were reported to have gone "above expectations," with both the government and the LTTE agreeing to curb the violence and to hold further talks on April 19-21.

In the meantime, LTTE resumed attacks against the military in April beginning with a Claymore anti-personnel mine attack on military vehicles which killed 10 navy sailors on April 11. The following day, coordinated bombings by rebels and rioting in the north-eastern part of the country left 16 dead. First, Claymore anti-personnel mine exploded in Trincomalee, killing two policemen in their vehicle. Another blast, set off in a crowded vegetable market, killed one soldier and some civilians.

In light of this violence, the LTTE called for a postponement of the Geneva talks until April 24-25, and the government initially agreed to this. Following negotiations, both the government and the rebels agreed to have a civilian vessel transport the regional LTTE leaders with international truce monitors on April 16, which involved crossing government-controlled territory.

However, the situation took a dramatic turn when the Tamil Tigers canceled the meeting, claiming not to have agreed to a naval escort. According to the SLMM, the Tamil rebels had previously agreed to the escort. This led to Helen Olafsdottir, spokesperson for the SLMM saying, "It was part of the agreement. The rebels should have read the clauses carefully. We are frustrated."

On April 20, 2006, the LTTE officially pulled out of peace talks indefinitely. While the outfit stated that transportation issues had prevented it from meeting the regional leaders, some analysts and the international community held a deep skepticism, seeing the transportation issue as a delaying tactic by the LTTE in order to avoid attending peace talks in Geneva.

The Norwegian mediators were now mere spectators. Sri Lanka was sitting on a powder keg, waiting to explode any moment.

Prabhakaran and his intelligence chief Pottu Amman were meanwhile plotting to deliver a massive blow to the military.

The LTTE leader had surmised that Gen. Fonseka was the likely danger man for the outfit.

So, true to his style, Prabhakaran decided to kill Fonseka.

On April 26, 2006, he sent a female "black Tiger," or a suicide cadre to kill Sarath Fonseka.

The planning, in true LTTE style was, meticulous.

The bomber, later identified as Anòja Kugenthirarasah, apparently faked a pregnancy and attended prenatal maternity classes at a military hospital located inside the Army headquarters for three weeks. She observed the Army commander's movements, his timings and the route that he took to his office and back home everyday.

On 26th April, as Fonseka left office for lunch, Anoja tried to get close to his car but a motorcycle outrider, driving ahead of the cavalcade noticed her suspicious movement and kicked her out of the way.

Unable to get any closer, the female bomber blew herself up, killing eight of the Army commander's bodyguards in the convoy and seriously injuring Fonseka and 27 others. The Army commander suffered grievous abdominal injuries. But over the next three months, Fonseka pulled through after surgery in Colombo and then in Singapore.

The attack inside the army headquarters was reason enough for Rajapaksa to abandon the pretence of a ceasefire.

The gloves were now off.

In retaliation, Sri Lankan Air Force planes bombed LTTE positions in the east and the north.

The failed assassination, in a way also marked the beginning of the end for Prabhakaran and plunged Sri Lanka into Eelam War IV.

CHAPTER 3

Eelam War IV Begins

The peace negotiations were now in tatters. I remember landing in Colombo a day after the failed attempt on Fonseka's life.

The Sri Lankan capital was on the edge. Security had been stepped up at all key locations in Colombo.

The Sri Lankan Air Force Kfirs were already pounding the East. When I reached Colombo a day after the failed attempt on Fonseka's life, war looked inevitable. But much of the skirmishes were still confined to the eastern areas of Trincomalee and Sampur.

Two days later, when and I Sukumar, my cameraperson colleague reached the Sampoor areas, hundreds of Tamil civilians were streaming out, fearing escalation in clashes. The aid agencies—ICRC, UNICEF, UNFPA—were all rushing in to help the displaced people. But the Sri Lankan Army and the LTTE had squared off and were deployed eyeball to eyeball.

We had to cross two check points—one manned by the Sri Lankan Army and the other by the LTTE cadres—before entering Sampoor.

There were tell-tale signs of air force bombing. The LTTE was busy mopping up the debris but fighters were also priming for a fight. LTTE sources had told me to meet S. Elilan, the outfit's political head in the Trincomalee area.

After much effort, we finally located Elilan at a remote location. Since he spoke only Tamil but understood English, Sukumar's knowledge of Tamil came in handy. As we sat down for an interview, Elilan predictably blamed the Sri Lankan army and air force for causing civilian deaths. In a long diatribe, he described Sri Lanka's attempts to break the truce. He said 15 died and 25 were wounded during a 16-hour bombardment, when 600 rockets and a dozen 500-pound bombs landed on an area held by the Liberation Tigers of Tamil Eelam (LTTE) in northeastern Sri Lanka.

"Only civilians were affected. We had advance warnings of the attacks so we warned everyone and they moved to safer places," he said. Elilan, unarmed and dressed in civilian clothes, said 26 houses had been destroyed but the final number damaged was still being assessed. He blamed the government for using aircraft, multi-barrel rocket launchers and artillery fire.

The military claimed that it was acting in self-defence, after Fonseka was attacked.

Elilan, however flatly denied the outfit's hand in the attempted assassination of the Army commander.

This was true to form.

In the past too, the LTTE had always disassociated itself from failed attacks while claiming credit for successful killings.

Throughout the interview, armed men hovered around. Across the street too, several young men, some in uniform, others wearing a *lungi,* but all armed with an assortment of weapons milled around.

"The situation is war-like. People are being killed by bombs and artillery fire. You can't say there's peace in Sri Lanka anymore," Elilan said as a parting shot.

Peace was indeed fragile but the war had not started yet.

Little did we know at that point that war would begin in less than three months.

And the spark was provided by water!

On July 21, 2006, the LTTE closed the sluice gates of the Mavil Aru (Mavil Oya) reservoir in Trincomalee district of the Eastern Province.

Geographically, Mavil Aru is located in an ethnically sensitive area where all the three communities in Sri Lanka—Sinhala, Muslim and Tamil—have their presence. Since the villages of all the three communities are located in close proximity to each other, any operations in this area would impact all the three communities.

Strategically too Mavil Aru is important.

Located south of the Mutur bulge that dominates the entry into the Trincomalee port and naval base, Mavil Aru has always been a point of confrontation between the LTTE and the government forces. In the past, the LTTE had dominated the area to pose a real time threat to the Sri Lankan navy base and free naval movement. The highway A-15, linking Trincomalee and Batticaloa areas also runs along this coast.

The closure of the reservoir cut the water supply to villages in government controlled areas. Nearly 30,000 people were deprived of their main source of drinking water. Vast paddy tracts dependent on Mavil Aru waters were also affected.

Initially, the government sought help from the ceasefire facilitators, the Sri Lanka Monitoring Mission, to resolve the deadlock. But the Tigers refused to relent.

Left with no other alternative, President Rajapaksa decided to take the bull by the horns.

Declaring that supply of water was a non-negotiable fundamental human right, Rajapaksa warned the LTTE: "If any one tries to obstruct it by laying down conditions, the Government will do everything within its means to overcome such obstructions and cater to the people's needs."

As luck would have it, just two days before launching Operation Watershed, the mission to secure the release of Mavil Aru from the Tiger hold, Army Chief Sarath Fonseka was back from Singapore after fully recovering from injuries sustained during the failed assassination attempt on him in April.

For the President, Fonseka's return was obviously a big boost.

The Army was told to act and open the Mavil Aru sluice gates by force if necessary.

After the failed negotiations the Air Force attacked LTTE positions on July 26, and ground troops began an operation to open the gates.

Gen. Fonseka decided to deploy one infantry battalion with an element of commandos to launch the initial assault.

Operation Watershed had begun.

As two companies set out from the Kallaru army camp to reach the Mavil Aru anicut a few kilometers away, they came under intense mortar fire. In anticipation of such an attack, the LTTE had already built T-shaped trenches from where they, the Tigers were bringing down accurate fire on the advancing Sri Lankan troops.

The firepower of the Tigers on the first day was so heavy that five infantry soldiers and two commando officers died in action. The troops were therefore forced to wait until the Tiger firepower gradually diminished. A day later, the troops managed to reach the west bund of Mavil Aru.

The operation to reach the sluice gates, however, proved much more arduous than first anticipated. The Tigers put up stiff resistance and the open terrain made progress difficult. The advancing troops were then provided with air cover and artillery fire. Simultaneously, in an attempt to put pressure on the LTTE, the Sri Lankan Air Force bombed targets in Tiger areas in the northern and eastern parts of the island.

The LTTE on the other hand, opened up more fronts to divert the troops' attention. On August 1, 2006, 18 soldiers being rushed to the area as reinforcement were killed when the bus they were traveling in was caught in a Claymore mine attack on the access road to the Kallar canal.

The most daring but once again an unsuccessful LTTE attack was to come later that afternoon.

A troop transporter ship with 800 soldiers on board was traveling from Kankesanturai harbor in the extreme north to Trincomalee. These soldiers were going on leave. The vessel, Jetliner, was hired on lease from Indonesia and was barely one month in service when it came under a suicide attack by nearly two dozen LTTE small boats. The Sea Tiger assault prompted Air force Kfirs and helicopter gunships to hover over the area while the navy's attack craft took up positions to face any eventuality.

The navy however managed to turn the passenger ship around and avert a deadly attack by turning into the inner harbor. Naval crafts providing security for the carrier sunk three Tiger boats and damaged another two. Thereafter, the Tigers shelled the naval base close by from their positions south of the Trincomalee bay. Several 122 mm artillery shells fell on the camp and four naval ratings were killed.

The next day, the Army camps in Kattaparichchan, Selvanagar and Mahindapura located south of the Trincomalee harbor came under attack. Several hours after the assault on the camps, the Muslim-dominated coastal town of Muttur also came under Tiger attack. Despite fierce fighting, the Tigers infiltrated into the town and occupied some Government buildings for some time. The army however launched a full blooded assault to reclaim total control of the town even as civilians fled in hordes.

At least 10,000 were rendered homeless by the fighting and aid agencies like the ICRC said that hundreds had been stranded on the roads leading from Muttur and were running low on food and water. Several hundred people were trapped in the town itself. Fifteen died when a shell landed in a school that they had sought shelter in and another 20 were killed due to shell fire while fleeing the town, according to ICRC.

By August 4, when the fighting was at its worst, all aid agencies, including the ICRC, pulled out due to security concerns. That day the Army declared that it was in control of the town and had killed more than 200 LTTE cadres. The Tigers also claimed that they had killed more than 100 Government troops.

The fighting continued for another four days. Eventually, the sluice gates were reopened on August 8. The Sri Lankan military had scored the first brownie points over the LTTE by conducting what it termed an "operation for humanitarian purposes."

Isolated battles continued over the next few days, but the LTTE was forced to give up its offensive due to heavy casualties.

After the setback in Mavil Aru and Muttur, the LTTE intensified attacks on the naval base in Trincomalee from its Sampoor stronghold.

Located across the Kottiar bay, Sampoor was under government control until the February 22, 2002 Ceasefire Agreement.

But during the truce period, the LTTE started setting up camps around the Sampoor area because of its strategic location giving the

LTTE a vantage point to fire long range artillery targeting Trincomalee and China bay across the Kottiar bay.

In April 2006, when I happened to visit Trincomalee, I had to go all the way to Sampoor to meet S. Elilan, the LTTE's regional political head since he was based in the area. The Tigers had set up full-fledged administrative machinery with a police station, courthouse, bank and tax offices functioning like government offices at Sampoor.

Between 2002 and 2006, the Navy had in fact alerted the government that the LTTE had occupied key strategic locations that would threaten the Trincomalee harbor in the event of hostilities breaking out again. But the military headquarters had chosen to ignore the warnings.

Now, as Mavil Aru fell to the Army, the Tigers were targeting the Trincomalee harbor with artillery fire.

Realizing the urgent need to neutralize the LTTE's presence in Sampoor area, the Army commander ordered an assault on the Tiger bases there.

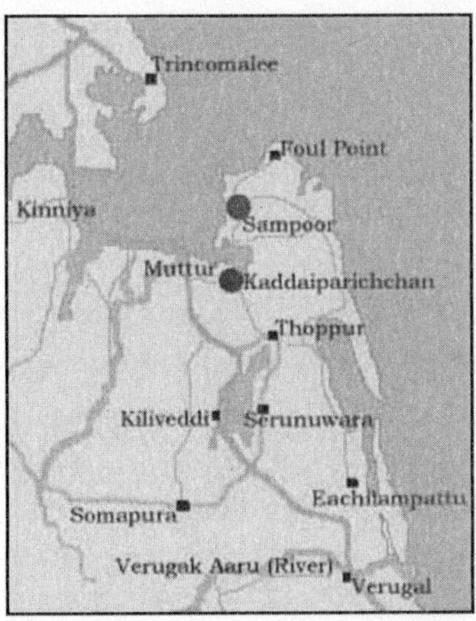

So on August 28, 2006 the Sri Lankan military launched an operation to retake the LTTE camps in Sampoor and the adjoining Kaddaiparichchan and Thoppur areas. After days of artillery shelling and aerial bombardment a major three-pronged military offensive began.

According to the Sri Lankan military, three advances were made from three different directions. The first was in fact a dummy operation with troops marching away from Sampoor instead of going toward it. The maneuvre was designed to deceive the LTTE.

Two infantry battalions, the 8th Sinha Regiment and the 6th Gajaba Regiment were tasked with spearheading the thrust. They were supported by elements from Special Forces.

In the months to come, this pattern of deploying special force elements in support of the infantry was to become a regular feature throughout Eelam War IV.

The LTTE forces were led by Col. Swarnam, the military commander of the Trincomalee district.

As ground troops began to advance, naval gunboats along the coast of Ilakkanthai began shelling the Muthur East littoral region. Artillery shells were fired regularly from the camps at Kattaiparichan, Selvanagar and Thoppoor towards the LTTE strongholds.

Simultaneously, the naval basc at the Trincomalee harbor and army camp at Monkeys Bridge began firing long range artillery as well as multi-barrel rocket launchers along the Kottiaar bay towards the Sampoor coast.

Sri Lankan Air Force Kfirs and MiGs too got into the action and began bombarding LTTE-controlled areas in Muthur East and Eechilampattru-Verugal regions.

Caught by surprise, the Tiger engaged advancing Army troops in the general area of Thoppoor at the crack of dawn. Through the day, fierce fighting ensued.

At first light on August 29, the battle recommenced across three fronts but neither side could break the stalemate. That's when the Army decided to bring in the armored cars and tanks in play. Aerial bombardment and shelling by naval gunboats meanwhile continued to support the ground troops.

The first breach in the LTTE defences occurred near a place called Pachanoor. The Tigers had well fortified positions near a jungle stream. After hours of fighting the Tigers started retreating across the stream and brought down heavy mortar fire on the advancing troops.

On the second day, the LTTE lost more men than the army, with radio intercepts suggesting at least 20 Tigers were killed as against half a dozen fatalities among the troops.

After two days of heavy fighting, the army paused to take stock and consolidate the minor territorial gains it had made. Several mines and booby traps had to be carefully cleared before any further advance. The LTTE too, it seemed, was conserving its resources. In the meantime, the LTTE's attempt to send in reinforcement by sea was thwarted by the navy when it sank a Tiger boat off Ilakkanthai.

The next two days witnessed intermittent artillery fire being exchanged. The Tigers were clearly in no mood to give up their control over Sampoor. The troops too stuck to their task.

Suddenly, the army was confronted with a new problem. Realizing that a major onslaught to capture Sampoor was imminent, frightened civilians had begun fleeing the area. Many escaped across the river to Batticaloa district. The administration was now stretched to accommodate these civilians and provide them with food and shelter.

On the battle front itself, the Army troops began gaining ground as the Tigers made a tactical retreat. On September 4, the military established a base in the Sampoor area after the LTTE admitted defeat and said its cadres "withdrew" from the strategically important town.

After nine days of fierce fighting, the troops recaptured Sampoor, Foul Point and Kattaparichan, leaving 120 Tiger cadres and 63 army troops' dead.

It marked the first significant territorial change of hands since the signing of the Ceasefire Agreement in 2002.

The immediate Tiger threat to Trincomalee was removed.

So why did President Rajapaksa choose to take on the LTTE in the East?

And why at that point?

He had two compelling reasons, one military and the other political.

In 2006, the eastern areas, it must be remembered, were not fully under the LTTE's control after Karuna had chosen to break away with his 6,000 loyal followers. So for the military it was easier to take on the LTTE at its weakest location.

Military expediency apart, Rajapaksa's decision was guided more by domestic compulsions and aided by the prevailing international environment prevailing in July 2006.

Elected on the support of an anti-Eelam platform, the President was under increasing pressure for months from the Sinhala parties like the Janatha Vimukthi Permana (JVP) and the Jathika Hela Urumaya (JHU) to confront the LTTE. The ceasefire was in tatters. For almost a year, the LTTE had stepped up its deadly attacks on the armed forces and killed civilians by the dozens. The brazen attack on the army chief inside the well fortified headquarters in the heart of Colombo had shaken the people's confidence in the government's ability to prevent such attempts.

The final straw was of course provided by the LTTE.

When the Tigers precipitated the crisis over Mavil Aru affecting the livelihood of 60,000 Sinhala peasants, President Rajapaksa found a perfectly valid reason to launch a military operation and satisfy the anti-LTTE lobby. And use of armed forces to resume water supply to farmers starved of Mavil Aru water was a perfect opportunity to showcase the government's concern for the poor.

From here on in fact, legitimate use of the armed forces to launch humanitarian relief was to become the Rajapaksa government's leitmotif over the next three years.

Internationally too, Colombo was now on a firmer wicket. Prabhakaran, through a series of ill-advised and ill-timed moves, had alienated several countries because of his ruthless methods in eliminating political opponents and blatantly violating the Ceasefire Agreement. The ban imposed on the LTTE by the European Union and Canada in May 2006 had added to the LTTE's problems.

Rajapaksa therefore rightly concluded that this was the best time to take on the LTTE. The military, which had in the past shown erratic results against the Tigers, winning some battles but losing many more, did not let the President down.

For the first time since 1999-2000, when the armed forces simply withered away after a fierce LTTE onslaught, troops stuck to their task even in the face of initial reverses. This clearly showed improved leadership qualities and higher morale. The coordination between the Army and the Air Force had also improved. In the past lack of synergy between the two arms had often slowed down operations.

The military of course benefitted from the LTTE's own tactical and strategic mistakes in the battle for Mavil Aru.

To begin with, Prabhakaran underestimated the new resolve among the military leadership as well as the troops. The LTTE also suffered because of lack of proper planning and execution. Hampered by lack of experienced military commanders in the East, the LTTE leadership tried to undertake a conventional battle even when it did not have adequate manpower to sustain such an approach.

After Mavil Aru and Sampoor's liberation, the message from Colombo was clear though: Unlike his predecessors, Mahinda Rajapaksa was willing to go the distance in taking the LTTE head on.

Sri Lanka was now firmly on the path to a full-fledged war, although officially neither side was willing to officially call off the ceasefire.

LIBERATING THE EAST

The recapture of Sampoor and the successful liberation of Mavil Aru had given the Sri Lankan military a new confidence. With the President fully backing the campaign, Army Commander Gen. Fonseka was now bent upon completely ousting the LTTE from the Eastern Province.

Fonseka and his Eastern commanders took three months to draw up a meticulous plan.

The Army resumed the offensive against the LTTE on December 8, this time in the Batticoloa district. The main objective was to hit the LTTE's main base in the area at Vakarai, a large backwater on Sri Lanka's east coast.

The Vakarai region encompasses the land north of Navalady Junction extending 50km to the Verugal River. The region's eastern boundary stretches to the shores overlooking the Bay of Bengal and the in the West, it has fertile agricultural land and forests. The Batticaloa-Trincomalee highway (A-15) also passes through Vakarai. Capturing Vakarai was therefore essential to Gen. Fonseka's plans to liberate the East but it was easier planned than executed.

After the fall of Mavil Aru and Sampoor, the Tigers had retreated southwards and had established several bases to fortify the defences leading to Vakarai. There were around 25 identified LTTE camps located between Kadjuwatta to Upparu on the way to Vakarai. In addition, the LTTE had set up three strong defence lines up to Panichchankerni Bridge each stretching about 3-6 km west from the eastern coast.

Undeterred, Fonseka, a veteran of many a battles with the LTTE in the past, had devised a new strategy: hit the enemy first at his strongest point. And in Batticaloa, the LTTE's strong defences were in the Vakarai area.

Later in May 2009, Gen Fonseka in fact explained to me why he adopted the new strategy: "Conventional military wisdom suggests that one should hit the enemy at his weakest point but knowing the LTTE's structure I thought if I could attack its strongest base right in the beginning of an operation—and win—half my task would be over since the LTTE did not have too much to fall back upon."

The Army commander had also guessed correctly that the LTTE was used to fighting across one battle front at a time. So he decided to do away with conventional warfare tactics.

With such strong defences in place, Gen. Fonseka and his local commanders realized that a conventional battle plan involving large, lumbering brigades or divisions would get bogged down for months in clearing and then holding on to LTTE areas. Instead, it was decided to launch several probing attacks across multiple points by small mobile teams. This was completely new, both to the Sri Lankan forces and to the Tigers.

This is where Fonseka's famous 8-man teams were born.

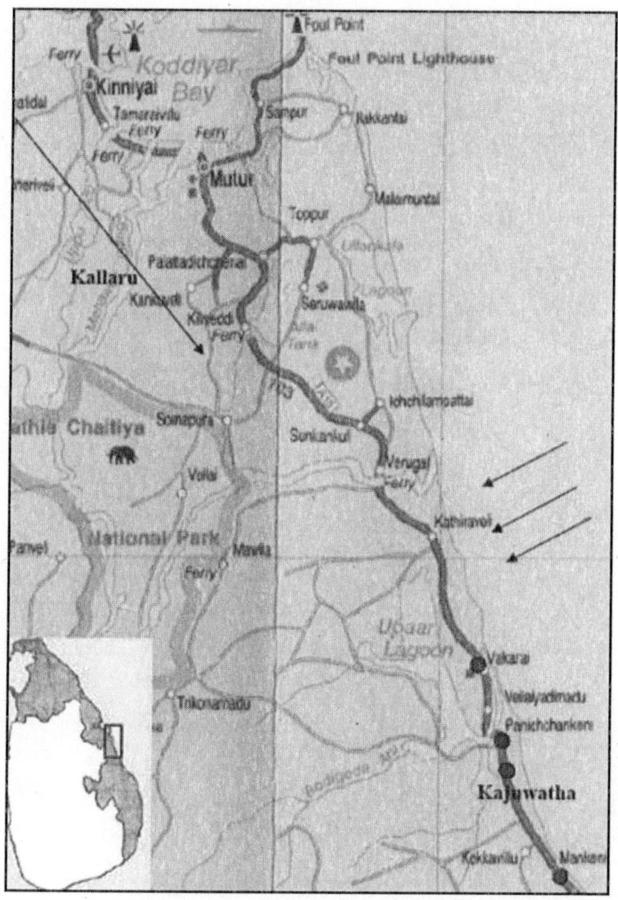

Comprising members of the Special Forces, the Army Commander ordered the formation of 8-man teams which would act as deep penetration patrols. Their task was to destroy as much LTTE's weaponry and bases as possible and retreat. Several such teams were dispatched to explore and attack LTTE held areas. This ploy allowed the formation commanders to gain valuable intelligence on LTTE's strongholds, its cadre strength and the kind of defensive positions it had built up even before commencing the main operation.

Fonseka of course also had to factor in the presence of a large number of civilians living in the area before launching an all out attack on the LTTE.

Since the presence of civilians was a major constraint, the Army sent out the elite Long Range Recee Patrol (LRRP) teams to keep the LTTE busy with a series of surprise attacks and allow civilians to escape to government controlled areas. The LRRP attacks were carried out in different locations forcing the LTTE to disperse its cadres in different directions. With the LTTE busy fighting across disparate locations, it was difficult for the Tigers to stop or control the civilian outflow.

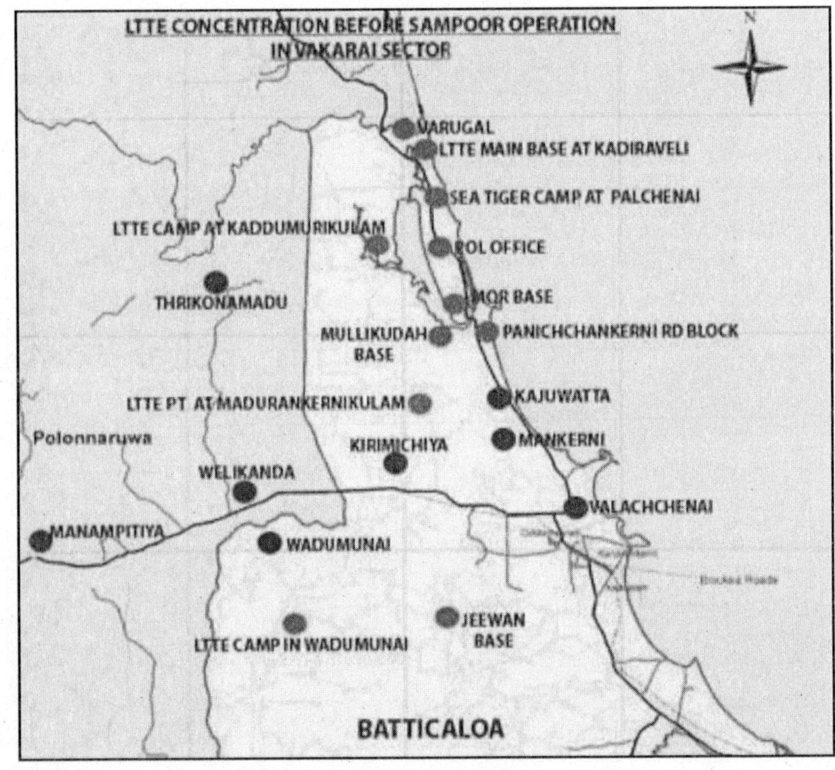

After two months of probing attacks mainly carried out by the 8-man and the LRRP teams, the army launched its first conventional attack on 4th December 2006. The troops advanced in three fronts capturing 15km territory inside the Trikonamadu jungle. Three LTTE bases were completely smashed during this phase of the operation.

Over the next five days, three successive assaults were unleashed from three different directions. One team of Special Forces attacked from Trikonamadu area and infiltrated 12km into the LTTE dominated areas crushing the Tiger camps in Thonithandamadu. Two LTTE bunker lines were captured.

By 10th December, when the first phase of the coordinated Special Forces Operation got over, infantry troops in small groups marched into the newly captured territories and consolidated the Army's hold. The arrival of over 21,000 civilians into government controlled area was an added bonus for the army.

As the battles on the field intensified, a parallel fight for media space between the Sri Lankan State and the LTTE also began in right earnest.

At the time, information about Army operations in Sri Lanka was being controlled from Colombo by a brigadier rank army spokesman, Brig Prasad Samarsinghe. A pleasant and helpful man, Brig Samarsinghe would share the latest information as soon as he received the input from the field. But he had his limitations since the armed forces in Sri Lanka like in most south Asian nations, were not geared to meet the media's constant need for immediate updates from the battle field. The military had simply not given enough attention or earmarked adequate resources to what is now known as Information Warfare.

The LTTE, on the other hand, was well served by the Tamilnet.com, a website run by a very resourceful and well-informed Tamilian named Dharmaratnam alias Taraki Sivraman. Tamilnet.com had access to the top leadership of the LTTE and its reporters had excellent field contacts across the island.

As a result, Tamilnet.com and by default the LTTE, used to win the battle for media space hands down those days.

In December 2006, when the LTTE was on the backfoot in the East, the Army was barely publicizing its feats but the LTTE, through Tamilnet.com was giving out detailed reports from the conflict area. Take this report by Tamilnet.com on 19 December 2006 for instance.

It said, in a report entitled: Humanitarian situation worsens in Vaharai:

"More than 20, 000 civilians continue to stay in temporary refugee camps at schools and surrounding houses in villages Kathiraveli, Vammivedduvan and Palchenai in Vaharai region amid acute shortage of food and humanitarian supplies, a local NGO official told TamilNet. Many families from Vaharai were forced to leave behind their grandparents who were unable to walk long distances.

The International Community has been increasingly criticized by the Tamils for maintaining silence, and for directly or indirectly supporting Sri Lanka's military strategy of forced eviction of Tamils from Vaharai region.

Sri Lanka Army, from Kajuwatte camp fired artillery shells towards Kathiraveli Monday at 9:05 p.m. 7 civilian houses were damaged.

5 SLA soldiers were wounded when LTTE fired in retaliation on the Kajuwatte SLA camp. The injured troopers, S.M.Kumarasiri, 42, K Wijesinghe, 33, M Rajakaruna, 36, M.K.Herath, 26 and S.L. Kumaradasa, 31, have been admitted to the Polonnaruwa hospital, sources from SLA Valaichenai Brigade Head Quarters sources said.

Tamil Rehabilitation Organisation official, S. Moorthy said elderly persons, left behind in schools and Vaharai hospital, need caretakers..."

By contrast, the defence ministry and the army did not have any dedicated website or an information centre at that point which could have given its side of the story or countered the Tamilnet.com reports.

Six months down the line however, the situation would undergo a dramatic change after Sri Lanka's Defence Ministry set up a Media Centre for National Security (MCNS).

But to get back to the Operations, by end of December 2006, the Sri Lankan army claimed to have killed at least 300 LTTE cadres, including a couple of senior leaders. The formation commanders attributed the high success rate to the innovative tatics of using Special Forces teams as "advance parties." Soldiers from the 1, 2 and 3 Special

Forces had done a commendable job for the army. But their job was yet only half done.

The Tigers, the army realized, had placed its heavy artillery guns close to the Vakarai General hospitals. The guns were firing incessantly from the civilian areas and from close to the hospital making it difficult for the Army to retaliate.

So for a fortnight, a lull descended on the eastern battlefront.

As the army was planning for resumption of operations in Batticaloa, an elite police commando team called the Special Task Force (STF) launched a major operation in the Kanchikudichchi Aru area of the neighbouring Ampara district on January 4, 2007.

This area was considered a vital LTTE stronghold since the Tigers had established more than a dozen bases to train and recruit combatants and store heavy weaponry and equipment.

The commandos recovered a large quantity of arms and ammunition, coffins, a large number of anti-personnel mines, satellite and radio receivers, global positioning systems, power generators, boats with name and logo of the NGO "Save the Children," tents with the logo of "UNHCR" and a fully equipped hospital donated to the militants by a Dutch NGO named ZOA Refugee Care.

The STF operation, code named "Niyathai Jaya" (victory assured) was especially satisfactory for the police commandos since it was in this area that the LTTE had executed 640 policemen way back in 1990 after they had surrendered to the LTTE.

Back in Batticaloa, the Army resumed its pincer movement against the remaining LTTE strongholds and after four days of intense battles, captured the Vakarai town.

Routed in the battle, LTTE cadres started fleeing towards the jungles of Thopiggalla area, leaving behind several weapons. Two of its top leaders, Swarnam and Nagesh too escaped the Army's dragnet.

There was no stopping the Army now.

In April 2007, the Sri Lankan troops also captured the strategic A-5 highway which had been under LTTE control for 15 years.

The LTTE's already diminishing presence in the east was reduced to a mere 140 square kilometres of jungle land in Thoppigala.

By June 2007, the troops had reached Baron's Cap in the Thoppigala jungle area. The LTTE's 'Beirut' base, the heart of the outfit's operations in Batticaloa sector for a long time was overrun by troops of 2nd Commando Regiment on June 11. The previous day, troops had captured four LTTE camps in Pankudaweli North, and Naarakmulla South.

Jubilant troops of the 2 and 3 Commando Regiments, 6, 7, 8 and 9 battalions of the Gemunu Watch, 1 Sinha Regiment, 10 Gajaba Regiment, an engineers, armored and artillery regiment each, all had contributed to the victory in Thoppigala.

The triumph marked the liberation of Thoppigala after 14 years of Tiger dominance.

In less than a year since Operation Watershed, the mission to liberate Mavil Aru had been launched in June 2006, Sri Lankan forces had done what many thought was impossible: Evict the Tigers completely from the East.

For President Rajapaksa, a calculated gamble had paid off. Several factors worked in his favor but the biggest contribution came from the Fonseka-Gotabaya duo.

Chapter 4

A Lethal Combination

When Mahinda Rajapaksa won the Presidential election in November 2005, he had a family visitor from the United States. Gotabaya Rajapaksa, the newly-elected President's younger brother had specially flown in all the way from Los Angeles to join the family celebrations.

Gotabaya had migrated to the US in 1992 to start a new life as an IT professional in a law school in LA. Comfortably settled in America, Gotabaya, it seemed had permanently left behind the memories of his first career as an officer in the Sri Lankan Army. He had quit as a Lt. Col. after completion of the mandatory 20 years' service.

America was now his permanent home. Or so it seemed.

But Mahinda Rajapaksa had other ideas.

Elected on an anti-LTTE plank, the new President had made up his mind to obliterate the Tamil Tigers when he took office.

And he needed his brother's support to execute this plan.

The moment he took over as President, Mahinda Rajapaksa told his younger brother: "You can't go, you wait. I want you to take over as Defence Secretary." *(Mahinda Rajapaksa to* The Hindu *Editor, N. Ram, 7 July, 2009).*

So just like that, in an instant and with minimum fuss, Gotabaya Rajapaksa abandoned his plans to return to the US.

And took over what turned out to be the most crucial post during Eelam War IV.

Gotabaya had no previous experience as an administrator but as an army officer he had seen enough action to understand the requirements of the job.

Commissioned as a Second Lieutenant in the Sri Lankan army in May 1972, Gotabaya had risen steadily through the ranks to command the 1st Gajaba Regiment in the late 1980s.

Like all his colleagues at the time, Gotabaya had first hand experience of fighting the Tamil Tigers. In 1987, he had led his battalion in Operation Liberation, the offensive mounted to liberate Vadamarachi from LTTE. Later, he was involved in Operation 'Strike Hard' and Operation 'Thrivida Balaya' in 1990.

For two years before his voluntary retirement, Gotabaya served as the Commandant of the Kotelawala Defence Academy, the institution that trains young officers in Sri Lanka.

One of Gotabaya's closest colleagues during the field postings was another lieutenant colonel.

His name was Sarath Fonseka.

Commissioned in the 1st Sinha Regiment in June 1971, Fonseka had made a mark in the army with his daring exploits and unconventional leadership.

As a brigadier, Fonseka played a major role in wresting the Jaffna peninsula and town from the LTTE during the famous 'Operation Riviresa' in 1995.

Even as a young officer, Fonseka had showed exceptional courage, meticulous planning and dynamic leadership while taking part in different operations during the three previous Eelam Wars against the LTTE. Injured in action during 'Operation Yaldevi', Fonseka was twice appointed Commander, Security Force Headquarters, Jaffna, the highest post in the Northern Theatre.

By the time the Rajapaksa regime assumed power in Colombo in 2005, Fonseka, as chief of staff, was among the seniormost officers in the Sri Lankan Army and was poised to take over as the next army chief.

By a strange twist of fate, the two men—Fonseka, at the peak of his career as a professional soldier and Gotabaya, as some one who had the total confidence of the highest authority in the land—were back together again to fight the LTTE.

It was no surprise therefore that among the first decisions Gotabaya took as Defence Secretary was to appoint Sarath Fonseka as the new Army chief.

Both have contrasting personalities yet they complement each other perfectly.

Gotabaya is hardnosed, inflexible, uncompromising; a man of few words and fewer friends but also clearheaded.

Fonseka is voluble and volatile, fearless in his actions and his utterances; a soldier who leads by example.

And both agreed the LTTE had to be crushed militarily.

Both didn't mince words when it came to criticizing the LTTE or their supporters in Tamil Nadu or in the West.

Gotabaya Rajapaksa for instance was accused of adopting the infamous Bush doctrine—you are either with us or you are with the terrorists—and did not bother about niceties.

He was intensely focused on the job. It did not bother him if during the single-minded pursuit of the end result—destruction of the LTTE—he antagonised the media, international NGOs or even Government ministers in the West.

His strategy was not just to defeat the enemy on the battlefield, but also to destroy its support base. Gotabaya did not differentiate between those who provided money and services, such as safe houses out of fear and intimidation, and those who did so out of conviction. Both met with the same punishment.

For him, people who objected to 'disappearances' and extra-judicial killings were not human rights activists; they were 'anti-patriotic busy bodies' at best, or LTTE sympathizers at worst. The Defence secretary has also been accused of threatening journalists on several occasions.

But during both my two extensive interactions with him, Gotabaya denied threatening journalists or human rights activists or being against them. "I am not against the media, as you think; or opposed to liberals as others have accused me of. My basic objection is to the people who masquerade as media practitioners but in reality are supporters of terrorists (read LTTE). I have certainly acted against them but it is unfair to charge me with being anti-media," he told me.

Despite his clarification, relations between Sri Lankan media and Gotabaya remain frosty even after the conclusion of Eelam War IV.

During the war, Gotabaya Rajapaksa's contempt for media was bettered only by his disdain for Western governments who pressurized—unsuccessfully—Colombo to stop the war till the very end.

An angry and at times agitated Gotabaya lashed out against the Western nation in an explosive interview to me for NDTV, saying: "Sri Lankan forces did much better than all the forces everywhere in the world when it comes to civilian casualties. We took all precautions to prevent civilian casualties from the beginning to the end (of the war). If one talks of taking our military to a war crimes tribunal, before that you have to take US troops, UK troops, all those troops and all those leaders into war crimes (tribunals)."

"The UN or human rights organizations should first do those investigations and (then) talk about investigation here," he said. His angry reaction came after a concerted campaign was launched in the West to probe possible war crimes by both government troops and Tamil Tigers during the war, with a number of European nations trying to bring a resolution to this effect at a meeting of the UN Human Rights Council in the immediate aftermath of the war.

Sarath Fonseka was equally acerbic.

In the course of a lengthy interview in the state-run *Sunday Observer* in December 2008, General Fonseka lashed out at politicians in the southern Indian state of Tamil Nadu and their demands that New Delhi pressure the Sri Lankan government for a ceasefire with the LTTE. "If the LTTE is wiped out, those political jokers [in Tamil Nadu] like Nedumaran, Vaiko and whoever is sympathizing with the LTTE will most probably lose their income from the LTTE," he declared.

Vaiko, one of LTTE's staunchest political supporters in Tamil Nadu, had been vocal and aggressive in demanding Indian intervention in Sri Lanka.

Asked if the Indian government would be influenced by protests in Tamil Nadu, Fonseka commented: "I am confident that the Indian government is not interested in a ceasefire in Sri Lanka as they have listed the LTTE as a terrorist organization. They have already accepted

[LTTE leader] Prabhakaran as a criminal and given him the death sentence... [Indian] Prime Minister Singh has enough problems after the Mumbai terrorist attack. They are against the LTTE and nothing in favor of the LTTE would happen."

Predictably Fonseka's remarks provoked a political storm in India, sparking demonstrations in Tamil Nadu.

But in the end, Fonseka had the last laugh.

Vaiko and many others like him, who were loudly proclaiming support to the LTTE in an effort to win as many seats as possible in the Indian general elections in May 2009, lost badly.

No amount of political storm fazed Fonseka. In an interview to me three days after Prabhakaran was killed, he revealed that some western nations were trying to save the top LTTE leadership till the very end by calling for a ceasefire. "They were trying to do it in the pretext of saving civilians but any ceasefire at that time, any fool would realize it was not going to save any civilian but would save the bunch of terrorists who were there," he said.

In the backdrop of allegations that LTTE political wing chief B Nadesan and peace secretariat head S Pulidevan were shot dead in cold blood when they had approached the forces for surrendering, Gen Fonseka said "(in) the last 300-400 metres area we surrounded them, cornered them, ... Nadesan, Pulidevan they got killed there. Ten minutes before we were shooting at them, I think, some members had spoken to Secretary Defence and said this Nadesan wants to surrender and in 10 minutes we recovered his dead body. The bullets were going over his head, through his ears," Fonseka told me.

Fortunately for both Gotabaya and Fonseka, the President backed them to the hilt supporting the war on terror although publicly Mahinda Rajapaksa had offered to discuss and deliberate a peaceful solution with the Tamil Tigers.

But waging a war against the Tamil Tigers was not easy.

In the past, the LTTE had withstood several assaults on its strongholds and at times inflicted humiliating defeats on the Sri Lankan armed forces.

Given his vast field experience, Fonseka already knew that in 2006 his own Army lacked self-belief despite some spectacular victories in the past 20 years.

But he was also aware that the LTTE had become an overconfident, somewhat bloated force, complacent in the belief that the Sri Lankan state lacked the will to sustain a long military campaign.

As Army Commander, Fonseka needed to turn these concepts and beliefs on their head. Within two months of taking over, Fonseka started imposing his own vision on the Army. He knew he needed numbers to sustain a prolonged campaign. So he decided to recruit more soldiers. He asked for weapons, he asked for more training slots for his officers and men. The President and the Defence Secretary met the demands forthwith.

In 2007 alone 40,000 new recruits joined the army. Negotiators traveled across the globe to buy arms. Czechoslovakia, Ukraine, China, Russia, Pakistan and even the United States sold arms to Sri Lanka in large quantity.

By beginning of 2006, Fonseka had given himself three years to achieve the end objective of defeating the LTTE.

Fonseka in fact told me after the end of Eelam War IV: "I had set myself a deadline of three years to crush the LTTE. But I needed to change a lot of mindsets and had to shake up the army somewhat. When I took over, most officers had the mentality that we cannot win this war, as had been the case in the past three Eelam Wars. But my belief was that with the right strategy and right selection of meritorious officers at every level, the LTTE could be defeated. So I personally selected capable Division, Task Force as well as Brigade commanders, not on seniority, but based on their past capabilities in the battlefield. I handpicked these officers on their merits. I placed my confidence in them. And as you can see they all performed spectacularly well."

If Fonseka was preparing and expanding the Army, Gotabaya was also concentrating on whipping the Air Force and the Navy into action. Despite his Army service the defence secretary knew that without total synergy between the three arms, it wouldn't be easy to pin down the LTTE.

Luckily for him, in Vice Admiral Wasantha Karannagoda and Air Chief Marshal Roshan Goonetilke, Sri Lanka had two outstanding officers, both proud of their service and both, somewhat like Fonseka, not tied down by the past experience.

Admiral Karannagoda, who was already the Navy chief when Mahinda Rajapaksa took over as President, has been credited with turning the largely ceremonial Navy into an effective force during Eelam War IV. Karannagoda in fact introduced a totally new doctrine in the Sri Lankan Navy and effectively blunted the deadly Sea Tigers, one of LTTE's most potent arms.

Amazingly, even the Sri Lankan Air Force which had largely functioned as an air transport arm of the Army, also transformed itself into an offensive force under Air Marshal Roshan Goonetilke. Goonetilke, whose father Harry was Air Chief in the 1960s, inducted state of the art equipment, ordered aggressive air raids deep into LTTE held territory and provided total support in casevac (casualty evacuation) operations to the army.

Mahinda Rajapaksa was extremely fortunate to have his brother as the Defence Secretary, ably supported by three outstanding commanders.

For the LTTE, the Gotabaya-Fonseka-Karannagoda-Goonetilke combination proved to be more lethal than it imagined.

GETTING READY FOR THE NORTH

On 19 July 2007, a week after the Eastern Province was freed, President Rajapaksa celebrated the victory in Colombo's Independent Square. In a tradition reminiscent of ancient Buddhist tradition of celebrating a military victory, Army commander Gen. Fonseka presented a plaque inscribed with the message of conquest of the Eastern province to Rajapaksa. A 21-gun salute heralded the victory.

But more than the pomp and show, it was Rajapaksa's speech that attracted the attention.

"There is no country other than Sri Lanka, where the criminal act of conceding a legal area of control to terrorists has been implemented through an agreement. It is the debunking of the myth of such an area of control, and the shattering into smithereens of the crowning terrorist fantasy of Eelam that our brave soldiers who captured Thoppigala have announced loud and clear to the entire world....

This blessed land will forever cherish, protect and value the fruits of the brave and courageous operation conducted by the Sri Lankan Security Forces to bring liberation to the people of the East; who for more than two decades were held hostage by the forces of vicious and violent terrorism. For many centuries the memory of this feat will inspire generations to come.

That this operation against terrorism was concluded with minimum harm to the people and least harm to the Security Forces stands out as an example of such action to all armies of the world that battle terrorism....

I observed some criticism of this victory. It said this was the majority race trampling on the minority race. Majority – minority? I do not like this interpretation. We are the Sri Lankan Nation.

The LTTE should even now accept the reality that it is not possible to bring liberation to the Tamil people through guns, bombs and cyanide capsules."

The triumphant tone was understandable. Since 1983, the government's control in the East had been tenuous at best. Rajapaksa was aware of the historic significance of the event and was therefore making grandiose statements. Behind the pomp and the ceremony though, the government was already preparing to launch the operations in the north.

Prabhakaran was surely aware of these intentions so in his usual style, the LTTE chief decided to spring a surprise even when his fighters were retreating from the East.

It came in the form of an air attack.

No other terrorist group would have conceived and then executed such a brazenly daring offensive.

The first mission of what the LTTE called the Tamil Eelam Air Force, or TAF, took place on March 27, 2007.

An aircraft set off, presumably from a jungle airstrip in the north of the country, and flew south. Incredibly, the intruding aircraft was not detected till it reached its target, the air force base at Katunayake, North of the capital.

According to the Sri Lanka Air Force spokesman, the light aircraft made a sneak raid around 12.45 am and lobbed two 'explosives' on a hangar killing three airmen and injuring 15 others.

However, the LTTE had claimed two of its aircraft took part in the raid and dropped four bombs on the target.

Later that day, the Tamilnet website published several photographs of the LTTE air force.

In two of the photographs taken in daylight, seven LTTE airmen in blue uniform were shown posing with Prabhakaran.

Three photographs showed views of four bombs under slung on the aircraft. This photograph was presumably taken ahead of the bombing raid.

Similarly, the tailfin and the body of the bomb showed they were probably improvised locally. A sixth photograph showed two pilots sitting in the open cockpit of a four-seat aircraft.

The air attack on March 26 came even as the Sri Lankan forces were in the process of ousting the LTTE from the East. It was clearly designed to boost the morale of the Tigers and demonstrate to the world that the LTTE was capable of pulling a rabbit out of the hat.

LTTE military spokesman Rasiah Ilanthiraiyan commenting on the air raid said: "It is not only pre-emptive; it is a measure to protect Tamil civilians from the genocidal aerial bombardments by Sri Lankan armed forces."

The raid was however put in perspective by two of India's best known analysts, counter-terrorism expert, B. Raman, formerly of the Indian External spying agency, the Reasearch and Analysis Wing (RAW) and retired Indian Army Colonel. R. Hariharan who had served with the Indian Peace-Keeping Force (IPKF) in Sri Lanka for three years as its intelligence chief between 1987 and 1990.

In an article on a popular website, *rediff.com,* Raman said: "It was not only a reprisal air strike, but also a pre-emptive air strike to prevent an offensive operation, which the Sri Lankan Armed Forces are planning to launch in the Northern Province in order to liberate the areas under the control of the LTTE there. A fresh team of Pakistani counter-insurgency experts and air force officers has recently arrived in Colombo to assist the Sri Lankan Armed Forces in their planned operations in the Northern Province.

The war against the LTTE started by President Mahinda Rajapaksa after assuming office in November, 2005, with the help of Pakistan, has now entered a new phase."

Col. Hariharan, in a separate analysis said:

"Objective of operation: It could be only to assert that LTTE still remained a force to reckon with, despite the beating it has recently taken with the heavy loss of men and material. In the present operations so far, the Sea Tigers have not been able to outsmart the Sri Lanka Navy imposing further limitations on the LTTE capability. The Security Forces have flushed out LTTE from most of its strongholds in the east. They are now poised to launch offensive operations along the Mannar-Vavuniya area and along the frontlines in Jaffna. All these compulsions are perhaps forcing LTTE leadership to produce dramatic results to restore its rapidly dwindling credibility, particularly among the Tamils both at home and abroad. And probably a surprise air operation was chosen for achieving this objective.

Results of the air raid: The LTTE air operation, despite the limited results it produced, has demonstrated a new dimension of LTTE capability under adverse circumstances. Thus it is sure to boost the sagging morale of LTTE cadres and its supporters. On the other hand, Sri Lankan planners would do well to understand that LTTE still retained the technical capability to maintain, arm and fly the aircraft. Perhaps, they would like to consider this aspect in planning future ground and air operations."

Col Hariharan was bang on. The air raid did create a sensation worldwide.

The BBC reported: "Whatever you may think of their goals and methods, Sri Lanka's Tamil Tigers have always been innovative. Experts say the technology was rudimentary but effective. It was they who refined the suicide bomber, and used them to devastating effect. And what other insurgent groups can boast a naval wing? The rebels have boats armed with guns, known as the Sea Tigers. Now they have confirmed what Sri Lanka's government have suspected for a long time - they have an air capability too."

MR Narayan Swamy, a long time watcher of the LTTE, and author of two books on the LTTE said: 'Way back in 1983, Velupillai Prabhakaran, on the alert, rode a bicycle through Jaffna to oversee a spot near the university his colleagues had picked to ambush Sri Lankan troops. Few people knew him then, and fewer had heard of the Tamil Tigers. A quarter century later, the same man, now a legend, has made history by using Tamil ingenuity to transform two light aircraft into stealthy bombers to target the air base of his enemy right in the heart of Sri Lanka."

The Sri Lankan military establishment was deeply embarrassed, but its spokesman put up a brave face. Reacting to the attack, Brig. Prasad Samrasinghe said: "It's not a new dimension. They were constructing a runway about two or three years back. During the ceasefire agreement they have brought all these things. This is the first time they have come and they were successful in putting the bombs. But they were not successful as per the plan that they wanted as they couldn't destroy any air force facilities. Definitely this is not a major threat and it will be neutralized."

And sure enough, undeterred by the psychological setback because of the air raid in March, the Sri Lankan army had managed to liberate the East in less than a year after it had launched the Mavil Aru operations.

Now Fonseka and Co. were preparing for an even bigger mission. The Security Council, headed by the President and comprising Defence Secretary Gotabaya Rajapaksa, the Chief of Defence Staff and the three service chiefs, had given a green signal for the northern offensive.

More soldiers, airmen and sailors were being recruited. The target for 2007 was to enlist 40,000 more men in the army to take its strength to over 150,000 by end of the year. The military victory in the East did bolster the government's campaign as thousands of youth lined up to enlist in the defence forces.

Fonseka decided to raise three new offensive formations, called Task Forces. These new formations would be double the size of an infantry brigade (3,000 soldiers) but smaller than a full-fldged division (10,000 men). He wanted these newly raised forces to spearhead the thrust into Wanni, the heart of LTTE's main defences, from both south and the north.

But expanding the defence forces needs enormous amounts of money.

In 2006, Sri Lanka had a defence budget of nearly 700 million US Dollars. In 2007, the figure touched one billion US dollars. The government said it needed to raise the military expenditure mainly to pay salaries to the increased manpower.

PK Balachandran, veteran journalist and a long-time observer of Sri Lanka wrote in *Hindustan Times* in 2006: "The twenty-five year long military conflict between the Tamil insurgents and successive Sri Lankan governments has made Sri Lanka the most militarized country in South Asia with 8,000 military personnel per one million population. The figures for other South Asian countries were: Pakistan, 4,000; Nepal 2,700; India, 1,300; and Bangladesh 1,000."

The government was hardly going to be bothered about these figures involved as it was in a fight to finish against the LTTE.

The military success in the East had given a new confidence to the government and yet Colombo found itself at the receiving end of a barrage of criticism from the international media and human rights organizations. Even the majority of the local media was skeptical about the efficacy of waging a sustained military campaign.

That's when Gotabaya Rajapaksa perhaps realized that the government was winning the war against the LTTE but was losing the battle with the media.

No one knows if Gotabaya Rajapaksa or some other senior military official had actually studied the relatively new concept known as Information Warfare and Information Operations. But by August 2007, the government had decided to augment a small facility called the Media Centre for National Security (MCNS) set up about a year previously.

It was an incredibly well-timed decision.

CHAPTER 5

Joining the Media Battle

In all the three previous Eelam Wars, the LTTE had won the battle for media space hands down.

Prabhakaran had realized earlier on that he needed the media's support to effectively fight the battle of perception.

Almost instinctively he had assessed the media's inclination to support the underdog.

So he had systematically and selectively, wooed the media. Indian and western journalists were especially favored by the LTTE.

Prabhakaran was however careful in not overexposing himself. A premium was in fact put on direct access to him.

A mystique was created around his persona. Interviews with him were rarely granted. Those who were allowed to meet him were always reminded that they were being favored.

Over the years, Prabhakaran created a mechanism through which every LTTE victory in the battlefield was transmitted throughout the world instantly; every setback was underplayed. A worldwide network, aided and financed by the Tamil Diaspora made sure that the LTTE was never out of the limelight.

In absence of any counter-propaganda, the LTTE invariably came out on top in cornering maximum media space.

Remembers an IPKF veteran: "The LTTE had mastered the art of winning the propaganda war even way back in 1987-88. It had set up a system through which every clash and encounter was relayed back to Chennai or smaller towns in Tamil Nadu. Although we used to take a lot of care in avoiding collateral damage to civilians, the LTTE's propaganda machinery would go into an overdrive after every small incident giving the Army a bad press. There was no one to counter the blatant falsehood. No wonder Indian citizens rarely bothered about the IPKF. All that we got was criticism, thanks to the excellent PR machinery that the LTTE had set up."

The Sri Lankan defence forces too suffered a similar fate between 1990 and 2007 although an Army spokesman was used valiantly to try and match the LTTE PR strategy.

Right from the beginning, Prabhakaran emphasized the importance of keeping photographic and video records of every action that the outfit carried out. Of course that practice backfired when a camera that recorded the very last moments of Rajiv Gandhi's assassination in 1991, helped unravel the entire conspiracy that killed the former Indian Prime Minister.

Later in 2008-2009 too the advancing Sri Lankan Army found thousands of photographs that gave a rare glimpse into Prabhakaran's family life and his meetings with various visitors. One memorable album showed Tamil Nadu politician Vaiko wearing an LTTE uniform, firing weapons and chatting with a much younger Prabhakaran at various locations in an LTTE hideout! These images were later used by the Sri Lankan government to score some brownie points against Tamil politicians who were criticizing Colombo for its military campaign!

But in 2007, in the wake of the successful Eastern operations, the Sri Lankan government felt it was not getting its message across clearly enough.

Defence Secretary Gotabaya Rajapaksa then decided to provide more resources to MCNS and make it into one consolidated, comprehensive centre that would disseminate all information related to the defence forces and the day to day progress of operations.

Remembers Lakshman Hullugalle, who heads the MCNS as Director General: "When the Secretary Defence called me and asked me to set up this facility, we were starting from scratch. The idea was to have one centralized information centre which would provide timely and accurate information to anyone who needed it. We, of course had no experience and were up against a professional and sleek website like the Tamilnet which was in existence for many years before us. In fact, I remember a time during previous conflicts when all of us in Sri Lanka used to turn to Tamilnet to get the latest information! You can imagine the disadvantage that we started with."

It didn't take the MCNS too long to catch up and then overtake the Tamilnet and other assorted pro-LTTE websites and information networks.

The MCNS became the most important address for visiting and local media during the war. It functioned from a small, non-descript building in the heart of Colombo's high security zone but outside the Defence Headquarters.

All of us had to go there to register ourselves for a trip into the battle zone; we asked for and got war footage from the MCNS; and its website was updated so frequently that all the latest information from the war zone was available almost in real time.

Its hierarchy was very well structured.

Hullugalle, a trusted aide of the President, was the overall in-charge as Director General. Senior officers from the Army, Navy, Air Force and even the police provided the information from their respective services. As a standard practice, a cabinet minister, Keheliya Rambukwella, briefed the media once a week in his capacity as Defence spokesperson. Of course if some extraordinary event took place, the media would be invited for a hurried conference at the Centre's well-appointed but cramped press briefing room.

Hullugalle, a pleasant, accessible man, became the most well known face and voice from Sri Lanka during the war since all TV channels went to him for a phono-in and a byte whenever they needed an official update. And he obliged everyone.

The Centre functioned 24x7, updated *defence.lk,* an information-rich website, almost every hour and all key personnel, including the DG, remained accessible round-the-clock.

The basic idea was to negate the LTTE's propaganda machinery and create a firewall around the battle zone. The objective was two-fold: control and denial.

Control the flow of information and deny access to unpalatable journalists.

The MCNS demonstrated that it had grasped the essence of information warfare and was putting it in practice everyday.

Purely as a battle strategy, the MCNS functioning was very effective.

By putting in place this system, Sri Lanka virtually eliminated the possibility of any other source giving news to the information-hungry media.

Even the trips to the battle zone—I went on several of them—were beautifully orchestrated.

We were always asked to report at the airport before dawn.

There, after a thorough security check, we would board a Ukraine-built AN-32 plane, land at Anuradhapura, a historic town in central Sri Lanka, and then get transferred onto two or three waiting Mi-17 Helicopters. Cameras would start rolling the instant we were on board the choppers. A piece to camera or a sign off on board a helicopter after all gives that sense of realism to war coverage!

So inevitably, most of us TV reporters would record at least two or three stand ups before we landed at either Killinochchi or Paranthan, close to the battle. Another very subtle arrangement used to be in place at those locations. An assortment of armored personnel carriers (APCs) and jeeps would be waiting for us to be taken to the brigade headquarters or a location closer to the actual fighting zone.

Now, a ride atop an APC is a television reporter's delight. A sign off or a stand up on board an APC, which looks like a tank, but is not really a tank (but then how many people can discern or distinguish a tank from an APC!) would do very well for your own as well as the channels image, thank you. The viewer will certainly be impressed!

So all of us TV reporters used to clamber atop an APC, do our stand ups and then go for a briefing, which from TV's point of view, are boring anyway. A formation commander at a lectern, explaining tactics on a map is not great television, so we would wonder out in search of images that conveyed a war zone. Invariably we would find soldiers in various stages of battle readiness outside the briefing rooms: some would be resting, others would be cleaning their weapons; APCs and jeeps full of soldiers in their fatigues would be whizzing past. So cameras would be busy recording those images.

The point is: the Sri Lankan military had worked out what TV crews need and provided the props accordingly. I am not saying any other militaries would not have done it. But most military planners in the world would have been less subtle.

The media handling by the Sri Lankan state would in fact make for a fascinating study. Having realized that the LTTE in the past had made very good use of its access to international media in projecting its image as an outfit fighting for a separate homeland for Tamils, Sri Lanka decided to cut off the oxygen supply of media support to the LTTE cause and instead deluged journalists with timely information and restricted their access to LTTE-held area.

The local media was tamed through twin methods of coercion and appealing to their chauvinism. Those who refused to fall in line, were coerced, threatened and even killed (14 journalists lost their lives in Sri Lanka in the last four years) and all others were won over by a simple appeal: it is as much your war as ours, so please cooperate. Simultaneously, pro-LTTE blogs and websites like Tamilnet.com were made inaccessible inside Sri Lanka.

The result: a completely one-sided coverage of Eelam War IV.

As a student of media, the Sri Lankan strategy fascinated me.

They refined the lessons and practices adopted by the Americans in Iraq and Afghanistan and evolved their own model that shuts out every other contrary view.

But war is a dirty business and nations adopt tactics that suit them.

As a journalist, I was not happy being part of a one-sided coverage, but to be fair to the Sri Lankan state, winning the information war was as essential as gaining the military victory.

But winning the media war wasn't easy.

Recalls Hullugalle: "When we started MCNS, we realized the LTTE had excellent contacts with the international media. We virtually had none. So we opened a dialogue with the foreign media. Gradually we started providing them with timely updates. Many a times, the LTTE used to doctor footage of our attacks and give false information. We decided to counter such news by giving authentic footage immediately and before Tamilnet could put it up on its website. Indian media which really started taking interest in the war from 2008 onwards was friendly but Western media people remained hostile."

Hullugalle at least had some experience in dealing with the media. He owns the franchise of popular sports channels ESPN and Star Sports in Sri Lanka and has family interests in a FM radio station in Colombo.

But for a career Army officer like Brig. Udaya Nanyakkara, who functions as the Army spokesman, the job was totally alien.

"I was completely surprised when asked to take over as Army spokesman in August 2007. I am a shy, soft spoken man. My seniors know it; they have recorded this observation even in my ACRs (Annual Confidentail Reports), so I didn't think I was suitable for this job at all. Like a true soldier though, I decided to meet the new challenge head on once I was given the orders."

"I was of course helped by my predecessors in understanding the requirements of the job. I spoke with some senior media people too. One of the first things I realized was you can't and should not fight the media," the brigadier recalled with a chuckle.

"Very early on, I had decided that there will be no personal favorites. I was aware that this was going to be a 24 hour job. And I must say my family never complained. My wife took care of the household and looked after our teenaged children without bothering me even once," Brig. Nanayyakara said.

So how was it to deal with the ever-demanding media?

"Overall, not bad really though I must say some of you can be quite irritating. But I kept my calm, telling myself, 'don't get angry. That is what they want so that you may slip up,' in the end most of you understood that I was doing my job and was not hiding anything deliberately."

As someone who kept in touch with both Hullugalle and the Brigadier almost daily in the last six months of Eelam War IV, I know what Nanayakkara was talking about. Each time I called them for updates, both said they will get back if they didn't have a particular piece of information. Both could afford to say that since both had direct access to the people in positions of power.

Recalled Hullugalle: "I could get to the President and the Defence Secretary at any time for important matters." Concurred Brig. Nanayakkara: "I had been given the authority to interact with the Army Commander and even the Defence Secretary if the matter was important enough."

But more significantly perhaps, the Brigadier, an Engineer Regiment officer, who had commanded an infantry brigade in the past, had direct access to the field commanders. There was therefore no time lag in receiving the information and transmitting it to us media practitioners.

There were other novel methods used to share information. The websites, *defence.lk* and *army.lk* were updated almost every hour; an animated battle progress map helped understanding the geographical location of each battle, latest videos and still pictures from the battle fields were uploaded very quickly. This helped media practitioners to get clear, updated information almost in real time. By contrast, Tamilnet was left far behind. Sri Lanka was winning the media war, finally.

There is perhaps a lesson in all this for the Indian Armed Forces and especially the mandarins of the Indian Ministry of Defence.

In India, the media policy is still stuck in the requirements of the mid-20th century media when it was sufficient for the officials to hand out a bland press statement and still expect the information to be printed in next morning's newspaper.

The needs of the 24 x 7 media, even if the babus and armed forces officers in the South Block don't like it, are completely different. A small country like Sri Lanka understood the essence of handling modern, fast moving media hungry for instant information. And exploited the media to its advantage.

That a section of the Western, 'bleeding heart liberal' media targeted the Sri Lankan state for what it calls war crimes committed by the Sri Lankan Army, is in a way, a left handed compliment to its strategy of creating a bubble around the war zone in which no one could enter without the permission of the Sri Lankan military.

By creating the Media Centre for National Security, Gotabaya Rajapaksa had once again played a master-stroke. But his real test lay ahead.

CHAPTER 6

Lording Over Wanni

It was September 1, 2007. The Army was poised to launch its Northern campaign. Wanni, as the vast area in the North, dotted with thick jungles and mangroves is known, was Prabhakaran's lair. Over the years, he had gradually established the LTTE's iron grip over the area.

As the Sri Lankan Army prepared to storm his bastion, many old timers in the Army recalled that the civil war actually began with a comparatively small ambush by the LTTE in Jaffna in July 1983 in which 13 Sri Lankan soldiers, all Sinhalese, were killed.

That killing unleashed a backlash that was to set off a chain of events that consumed the nation in an orgy of violence over the next 26 years.

Sporadic violence was not new to Tamil-majority areas in the North of Sri Lanka. Since the mid-1970s, a new, impatient and firebrand crop of Tamil youth had started to harass the Sri Lankan police and other government servants through their hit and run tactics, looting a bank here and killing a policeman there in the Island's North.

Vellupillai Prabhakaran, the youngest son of a Tamil government servant was one of the many young men who believed in taking up arms against the discriminatory Sri Lankan state. He first established an outfit called the Tamil New Tigers (TNT) in 1974 and two years later on May 5, 1976 founded the Liberation Tigers of Tamil Eelam.

In the subsequent years several other armed groups like the Tamil Eelam Liberation Army (TELA), its political wing, the Tamil Eelam Liberation Organization (TELO), the People's Liberation

Organization of Tamil Eelam (PLOT), to name only a few, emerged. Many activists were arrested, some killed and many others just drifted away from the cause. But not Prabhakaran. He was determined to fight on for creation of Eelam no matter how long it took.

Unknown to the Sri Lankan state, the seeds of the future conflict were being sown in the Jaffna peninsula in the mid-1970s. But the agitation was largely confined to the Tamil majority areas in the North and parts of the East. In Colombo and in Sri Lanka's deep South, very few Sinhalas had the real inkling of the simmering discontent in the Tamil-majority areas.

The protests were localized until Prabhakaran and his group decided to ambush a Sri Lankan Army patrol codenamed "Four Four Bravo" killing 13 soldiers, all Sinhalas in one swoop. That was the first major attack by the "boys" on the Sri Lankan Army. Their death ignited a firestorm against the Tamils in Colombo.

As the bodies of the soldiers, some of them barely out of their teens, arrived in Colombo, violent mobs and not policemen seemed to rule the streets.

Wherever policemen were present, they looked the other way and at times participated in the looting and killing spree against the Tamils.

The events that followed that killing are still remembered with horror by Tamils in Colombo.

The retaliation by a section of the Sinhalas was disproportionately high.

Innocent Tamil who lived in Colombo for years and had nothing to do with the LTTE, were mercilessly massacred by Sinhala mobs, their houses looted, their business establishments completely destroyed.

Hundreds, some say, thousands of innocent Tamils were killed.

Over 100,000 Tamils, most of them from middle-class families lost everything they had and were forced to take shelter in refugee camps. Even Tamil prisoners in a high-security prison on the outskirts of Colombo were butchered by fellow Sinhala prisoners.

Several accounts of that time put the number of innocent Tamils killed during that terrible time, at anywhere between 400 and 3,000.

The anti-Tamil riots of July-August 1983 were to prove a turning point in the troubled history of Tamil-Sinhala relationship in Sri Lanka. The violent backlash only served to reinforce the view among the younger generation of Tamils that they had no future in a Sinhala-dominated polity of the Island nation.

The relations between the Tamils and majority Sinhalas, not always cordial over the years, were now beyond redemption.

Narayan Swamy in his book *Tigers of Lanka*, says: "The Tamil-Sinhalese ties, under increasing strain over the years, had finally suffered a near irreparable damage ... the two communities would now drift apart ... the riots truly heralded Sri Lanka's ethnic conflagration."

And kick started Eelam War I.

From then on, the beautiful Island Nation was witness to four bloody phases of brutal wars, dubbed Eelam War I, II, III and IV.

In May 2009, the Sri Lankan armed forces finally knocked out the once formidable LTTE but in the quarter century before that over 100,000 people—soldiers, LTTE cadres, innocent civilians on both sides of the divide—perished in the brutal bloodshed that consumed this impossibly beautiful island.

To understand why and how the Sri Lanka military managed to wipe out the Tamil Tigers, it is important to look back and briefly understand how the earlier battles were conducted. And why Prabhakaran managed to stave off the might of the Sri Lankan state for so long.

EELAM WAR I

Till 1983, the Sri Lankan military was largely ceremonial. With a combined strength of less than 40,000, the three wings—Army, Navy and Air Force—had very little role to play in the nation's affairs. Most of the officers came from prosperous, urban families. Many of them joined the forces after graduating from Colombo's best public schools and colleges. Much like the Indian Army officers in the 1950s, soldiering for them was more a way of life than a profession.

Remembers a former Indian General, who as a colonel, trained with some of the Sri Lankan Army officials at the Counter-Insurgency and Jungle Warfare School (CIJW) in Mizoram during the mid-1970s: "For our Sri Lankan friends, the stint in CIJW was a novel experience but something that they didn't take seriously. They knew that the intense, specialized counter-insurgency training was of no use back home." Little did they realize that in less than a decade, the situation in Sri Lanka would undergo a sea change.

Indeed by the mid-1980s, the Sri Lankan Army was forced to change its attitude. By early 1983, Tamil militant groups had become a realistic threat in the North and the East for the army to step in. The police were unable to cope with the increasing attacks by Tamil militants on government installations and against civilians. The innovative and unconventional methods adopted by the Tamil militants were taking a heavy toll on the law enforcers.

But it was not easy to transform a largely ceremonial Army into a fighting force.

In the years between 1983 and 1987, the Sri Lankan Army and the fledgling Navy suffered heavily.

The troops, not used to hardships or intense battles often got waylaid and trapped by the Tamil militants. Unsuspecting military convoys, unfamiliar with the terrain in the North and the East, often got blown up, killing scores of troops in the process. The 'boys' as the Tamil militants came to be known, on the other hand, used their knowledge of the area to maximum advantage employing landmines on the roads frequented by the forces to cripple their movement.

But no State takes too long to retaliate.

And in Junious Richard Jayewardne, Sri Lanka had a President who had come up the hard way in Sri Lanka's politics and was as crafty as they come.

He was not going to let a bunch of 'boys' get away with murder.

As a first step, in March 1984 he appointed Lalith Athulathmudali, an Oxford educated lawyer and rising star in Sri Lankan politics, as the country's first National Security Minister. Athulatmudali's task was clearly spelt out. He was told to take 'appropriate measures to strengthen, modernize and motivate the military to meet head on the challenge thrown at the Sri Lankan state by the Tamil militants.'

In the next three years, Athulatmudali did boost the military's strength and gave it free hand to deal with the Tamil militants.

But the carte blanche to the troops only served to harden the Tamil position since the Army's tactics matched the brutality unleashed by Tamil militant groups.

A vicious cycle of violence and counter-violence consumed the North. If Tamil groups were guilty of massacring innocent Sinhalas, the Sri Lankan Army was no less culpable in targeting hapless Tamil civilians when it failed to catch or kill the militants. The bloodletting went on unhindered, punctuated by an occasional ceasefire.

The widespread July 1983 riots against the Tamils brought India into the picture. Till then, New Delhi had studiously remained aloof from the Sri Lankan affairs.

But after the riots, India could not keep away given the reactions they evoked in Tamil Nadu.

Assuming the role of a mediator, India tried to bring the warring groups together at a peace conference in Bhutan's capital Thimphu. But despite its best attempts at a patch up, neither side could find a common meeting ground at the July, 1985 Bhutan meeting.

Once again violence resumed in the North and in the East and continued throughout 1986.

As 1987 arrived, the breakdown of the already fragile ceasefire was complete.

Sri Lankan Air Force jets bombed LTTE strongholds without bothering about collateral damage to the civilians. The LTTE, for once, was feeling the heat of a numerically superior and better equipped military force. Jaffna was under siege now and the LTTE did not know how to react to the situation. Food and fuel shortage hit the Jaffna peninsula as the Sri Lankan Army enforced a blockade.

India was however not willing to be a silent by-stander any more. Prime Minister Rajiv Gandhi sent his foreign minister Dinesh Singh to Colombo seeking to rein in the Sri Lankan Army's final assault on Jaffna. At first appearance, President Jayewardene was in no mood to listen to India's advice since a week prior to Singh's arrival, he had taken a public stand vowing to continue the military campaign to eliminate Tamil militant groups.

But in the wake of the meeting, the President quite unexpectedly announced a week-long ceasefire starting April 10, coinciding with Tamil and Sinhala New Year celebrations.

Peace was to last just for a week though.

What prompted the LTTE to massacre over 100 unarmed military personnel and their families when they were proceeding on leave on April 17 that year, will never be known but that carnage and a bomb blast in the heart of Colombo three days later set off a chain reaction.

An enraged President Jayewardene asked the Sri Lankan military to launch a 'fight to finish' campaign against Tamil militants and force them to surrender. Over 8,000 troops of the Army supported by the Air Force and reinforced by the Navy, commenced "Operation Liberation," a massive military surge against the LTTE strongholds in the Jaffna peninsula, a month after the Colombo bomb blast.

"The offensive began with seven Air Force aircraft each accompanied by two helicopter gun ships, strafing Jaffna. They dropped bombs weighing more than 50 kg. The Army-operated Radio Jaffna repeatedly urged the people to move into churches and temples to escape air tacks. Thousands of leaflets were also dropped from the air directing the civilians to take shelter likewise. Hundreds followed the advice, only to be bombed where they were supposed to be safe," Narayan Sawmy wrote.

The well fortified LTTE defences at Vadamarachchi, south of the strategic Elephant Pass collapsed in the face of the massive onslaught. As the troops marched in into the Jaffna peninsula, the LTTE fighters, including Prabhakaran, simply abandoned the area, leaving the civilians to face the wrath of the Sri Lankan Army. News reports of that time have chronicled how hundreds of young men in the 20s and thirties, picked up by the Army for interrogation never returned home. Death and destruction engulfed Jaffna town.

India was aghast. It had not expected President Jayewardene to pursue the military option and allow the civilians to be targeted in such a manner. Rajiv Gandhi's government drew up a two-pronged strategy. While it kept a channel open with the Jayewardene regime, India also looked at an option to intervene militarily.

In a show of force, on June 4, 1987 half a dozen AN-32 aircraft of the Indian Air Force, escorted by fighter jets air dropped over 25 tonnes of essential items over Jaffna for its beleaguered citizens.

Sri Lanka was livid. But in the face of an overwhelmingly powerful neighbor like India, it had no choice but to swallow the insult.

The largely symbolic air-drop under Operation Poomalai forced Messrs Jayewardene and Athulathmudali to scrap Operation Liberation. This also marked the end of Eelam War I.

But unknown to everyone, the end of Eelam War I was setting the stage for a bigger and bitter battle, this time between the Indian Army and the Tamil Tigers. Three years later, the Sri Lankan state would have the last laugh.

But all that was in the future.

For the moment India was aglow with what it thought was a major military-diplomatic triumph. By launching Operation Poomalai or Garland, India had made its point and sent a signal to the Tamils in Sri Lanka that only she could save them.

Hope sprang among ordinary Tamils.

Events moved swiftly thereafter. Within 50 days after the air drop, Rajiv Gandhi, aided by his pushy, overbearing High Commissioner in Colombo JN Dixit had drawn up an accord intended to settle the issue in the North and the East of Sri Lanka forever.

Instead, the Accord ended up sending Indian troops into an unknown territory without a clear politico-military objective in mind. And leave a near permanent scar on India's collective psyche.

President Jayewardene, smarting under India's unilateral move, did agree to sign the Indo-Sri Lanka accord on 29 July 1987.

Ironically, none of the parties was happy with the terms of the accord.

The Buddhist clergy and the majority Sinhala saw the accord as a prelude to the division of Sri Lanka on ethnic lines.

The Tamils, especially the LTTE, forced into accepting the accord, were also an unhappy lot. They felt short-changed since the terms of the accord did not fulfill any of their long-standing demands.

Ultimately, the Indian Peace-Keeping Force (IPKF), sent into Sri Lanka's north-east to disarm Tamil militant groups and particularly the Tamil Tigers, ended up fighting the LTTE.

It took nearly three years and a loss of 1400 gallant Indian soldiers for the government to realize its mistake in intervening in an alien land without a clear end-objective in mind. And as if to rub salt in the Indian wounds, the new leadership in Colombo under Prime Minister, later President, Ranasinghe Premadasa, consistently undermined the Accord. The instinctive survivor that he was, Vellupillai Prabhakaran in fact colluded with the Premadasa government to undercut the IPKF.

But to the credit of the Indian Army despite Prabhakaran and Premadasa's betrayal, it had considerably weakened the LTTE's military capabilities and demonstrated how a guerilla group could be tamed against heavy odds.

Two decades later, officers of the Sri Lankan defence forces were to acknowledge—in private—the contribution of the Indian troops in setting the stage for the decimation of the Tamil Tigers. But in March 1990 when Indian troops left Sri Lanka, no one would have imagined that violence—and another Eelam War—was about to start within three months.

EELAM WAR II

When the last of the IPKF contingent left the shores of Sri Lanka, President Ranasinghe Premadasa and Prabhakaran were gloating, but for different reasons.

Premadasa thought he had played a masterstroke by helping Prabhakaran drive out the IPKF and now the LTTE would accept a solution to the Tamil issue within the framework of the Sri Lankan constitution.

He had clearly underestimated Prabhakaran's cunning.

As far as the LTTE supremo was concerned, he had supped with the enemy (Premadasa) only to ensure that the bigger threat (India) to his ambitions was out of the way. Once the Indian forces went back home, dejected and disgraced, Prabhakaran resumed his armed campaign with a ferocity that singed the Sri Lankan nation-state like never before.

It was as if Prabhakaran was giving vent to three years of frustration and anger at being on the run from a well-trained and professional India Army.

Between June 1990 when he re-launched the war for Eelam and 1993, Prabhakaran not only captured large swathe of territory but also eliminated, through assassinations and murders, all those who had insulted him or had tried to use him.

The first of the major assassinations was that of Ranajan Wijeratne, President Premadasa's trusted man and deputy defence minister. Regarded as a hardliners in Sri Lanka's fight against the insurgency, Wijeratne had helped the President in crushing a Leftist rebellion by Sinhala youth in Sri Lanka's south in 1990 and was handling the military's push against the LTTE. Wijeratne had publicly vowed to finish the LTTE much in the same manner as he had put down the students' rebellion in the South. But the LTTE had other ideas. Wijeratne was blown to pieces in an explosion in Colombo's busy Havelock Street in March 1991 when he was driving to work in his armored-plated Mercedes car.

In April 1993, Lalith Athulathmudali, who was Sri Lanka's first National Security Minister, had almost brought down the LTTE to its knees before India foolishly intervened in 1987, was killed by the Tamil Tigers in Colombo. Less than 10 days later, Ranasinghe Premadasa, who had flirted dangerously with Prabhakaran, was killed by a suspected LTTE suicide bomber at a May Day rally in the Sri Lankan capital.

Prior to these two major strikes, Prabhakaran had also got rid of Sri Lankan Navy chief Clancy Fernando and chief of the Army's northern Command, Brig. Denzil Kobbekoduwa and a host of senior army officers in a land mine explosion.

But the assassination that earned the LTTE a worldwide notoriety was the killing of Rajiv Gandhi. The former Prime Minister, who had lost office in 1989, looked set to return to power in the summer of 1991.

Prabhakaran feared he would once again order a military intervention in Sri Lanka. So Prabhakaran and his intelligence chief Pottu Amman hatched a plot to kill Rajiv Gandhi.

Gandhi's assassination at the hands of a female suicide bomber in Tamil Nadu's Sriperumbedur town when the former Prime Minister was about to address a public meeting on May 21, 1991 was the LTTE's most infamous strike and as events were to prove later, its biggest strategic mistake.

By killing Gandhi, a popular and young (by Indian standards) political leader, the LTTE lost in one stroke, whatever sympathy it may have had in the Indian establishment.

But back in Sri Lanka, Prabhakaran had managed to establish a firm LTTE presence in much of Jaffna peninsula and large parts of Killinochchi, Vavuniya, Mannar and Mullaitivvu districts. In the East too, major portions of the Batticaloa and Trincomalee districts came under the LTTE control. Eelam War II had been a total success for Prabhakaran and his Tamil Tigers. The Tigers virtually had a state within a state and indeed introduced a visa system for those who wanted to enter their territory!

EELAM WAR III

By 1994, having established a de facto Eelam in its traditional strongholds, the LTTE was now in a position to dictate terms to Colombo. Prabhakaran was of course lucky that Chandrika Kumaratunga won the presidential election in 1994.

Kumaratunga, who's mother, Sirimao Bandernaike had the distinction of being the world's first woman Prime Minister in the late 1950s, was considered a dove among Sinhala politicians of the time. Hopes were riding high on her approach towards the Tamil issue. She had in fact won the elections on a peace agenda and weeks after she took office, Kumaratunga opened talks with the LTTE.

The President made it clear that her administration was willing to go more than halfway to meet the LTTE's demands. And for once, a war-weary nation was willing to back Chandrika Kumaratunga. But the peace offensive was to last less than a year. Inexplicably Prabhakaran decided to withdraw from the talks in April 1995. Attacks on Naval and Army convoys began almost immediately.

Eelam War III was on.

But unlike the earlier two editions, this war initially was not going Prabhakaran's way. For one, the LTTE was now defending a larger territory with few thousand fighters. And secondly, this time the war was initiated by the Tamil Tigers and not the Sri Lankan state, so the world was not as sympathetic to the LTTE cause as it was on previous two occasions.

OPERATION RIVIRESA

Kumaratunga called the Eelam campaign III as a "War for Peace," and justified the use of military means to bring the LTTE to heel after Prabhakaran withdrew from the negotiations.

So when in October 1995, the military launched its frontal assault on Jaffna under 'Operation Riviresa (Sunshine)', for once the international community could not really fault the government.

She had another compelling reason to authorize Operation Riveresa. After withdrawing from the peace talks, the LTTE had sunk two naval crafts in Trincomalee but more dangerously for the armed forces, unveiled a new weapon: the shoulder-fired anti-aircraft missile. In April 1995, two Sri Lanka Air Force Avro aircrafts were shot down in two days while flying over the Jaffna peninsula. Almost 50 officers and men perished. The SLAF was forced to suspend all flights to the peninsula. To add to the problems, in July, an army operation launched to expand the area around the sprawling Palaly airbase ended in disaster. Troops had to concede approximately 80 square km to the LTTE.

It is in this backdrop that Kumaratunga authorized what till then was the biggest military operation against the Tigers.

In many ways, Operation Riviresa was a precursor to the strategies adopted by the military a decade later in Eelam War IV.

For the first time, for instance, the military was given a clear politico-military objective. There was excellent equation between the chief executive (President Kumaratunga) and the military. And perhaps for the first time in Sri Lanka's recent history, the Army, Navy and Air Force displayed total synergy in their operations.

It demonstrated the new-found professionalism of the Lankan troops and their ability to fight a coordinated battle. A lot of planning preceded Operation Riviresa before it was launched on October 17, 1995 with over 20,000 troops collected at the gates of the Jaffna peninsula to evict the LTTE.

The Operation, commanded by Major General Rohan Daluwatte as Overall Operations Commander (OOC), involved three formations, the 51, 52 and 53 Divisions. The troops advanced astride the Jaffna-Point Pedro and Jaffna-Palaly Road axes. This advance was met with stiff resistance from the LTTE and it took the divisions almost a month to cover the 12-mile stretch since LTTE had prepared for the attack in advance by mining all roads into the peninsula and by creating defenses in depth with additional cadres from the Eastern Province.

Despite the admirable resistance put up by his cadres, it was becoming difficult for Prabhakaran to hold onto Jaffna.

He then took a strategic decision to vacate the peninsula of its entire population. For the LTTE the biggest triumph during those tough times was the overnight population transfer from Jaffna to south of the Elephant Pass.

Even assuming that the people were forced to leave Jaffna at gunpoint and settle in parts of Killinochchi and Vavuniya, it showed the LTTE's power and influence since 300,000 people, young, old, women and children vacated Jaffna in less than a fortnight. So when the Sri Lankan Army marched into Jaffna town after overcoming a spirited defence put up by the LTTE fighters, it found the town bereft of people except a few old and infirm citizens who could not move out with the rest of the population.

In the later years too, the LTTE would once again demonstrate its ability to force such large number of people to move with it. It is however a different matter that ultimately, the presence of such a large number of civilians contributed to the Tigers' downfall in the summer of 2009.

Two officers involved in the 1995 operation—Brig. Sarath Fonseka and Maj. Gen. Janak Perera—were to later become household names in Sri Lanka.

Fonseka, was the deputy commander of the 51st division and Perera led the 53rd Division. Fonseka went to become the Army Commander to successfully lead the Eelam War IV campaign and decimate the LTTE in 2009.

Perera, after retirement from the Army, took up a couple of diplomatic assignments before he and his wife were killed along with 30 others in a blast in the city of Anuradhapura in October 2008.

For President Chandrika Kumaratunga, seizing control of Jaffna after almost a decade of military reverses in the North was a high point but the triumph was to be short-lived.

Prabhakaran was not a man to sit idle. Having suffered a tactical defeat in Jaffna, he was already plotting to deal a crippling blow to the Sri Lanka Army.

The army of course expected a counter-offensive but not the ferocity of the counter-offensive. So when the attack actually came, the same Army which had displayed superb tactical acumen and sterling fighting qualities, failed to match the LTTE. It was routed by the Tigers in the subsequent battles, notably in the fall of Mullaitivvu and the loss of the strategic Elephant Pass.

OPERATION UNCEASING WAVES, 1996

On July 18, 1996 the LTTE launched a ferocious attack on the Sri Lankan Army base located in the town of Mullaitivvu on the north eastern coast of Sri Lanka. Code named 'Operation Unceasing Waves,' Prabhakaran had especially trained nearly 4,000 LTTE cadres for this attack. He was smarting under the Jaffna setback in October 1995 and was seeking revenge.

He had chosen the target carefully.

The army base at Mullaitivvu was spread over a large area and was bordered by the sea on one side. In 1996, the Mullaitivvu camp was the headquarters of 215 Brigade. Two of the three battalions under the brigade—the 7th Vijayabahu Infantry Regiment and the 7th Sinha Regiment—were also based in the same complex.

It was an isolated complex, far away from any other base in the vicinity.

As Prabhakaran primed his fighters for an important battle, the LTTE's intelligence wing, which had provided very accurate and effective tip offs in the past, told the Tigers' chief that two senior most officers—the commander and his deputy—of the brigade were not in station that day. This was the signal Prabhakaran needed to launch his attack.

The assault, in keeping with the classical convention, began at 1.30 a.m. on the 18 July, 1996. As the frontline LTTE fighters neutralized the sentries and watch parties, Army soldiers, resting in various mini-camps in the garrison rushed out to reinforce the defences. But the LTTE was prepared. Its second wave of fighters overwhelmed the reinforcements.

As the news of the attack reached the higher ups, the Army sought to send in extra troops from the nearby naval bases located at Vettilaikerni and Trincomalee. But the Sea Tigers were lying in wait for exactly such a possibility. They pinned down the troops and prevented them from getting out of the bases.

Back in Mullaitivvu, after hours of heavy fighting, the Tigers had reached the centre of the camp and captured artillery sites and armories.

By noon, the LTTE fighters had stopped firing, clearly waiting for nightfall before resuming the assault.

In the meantime, the Army dispatched a few hundred Special Forces troops to extricate the besieged soldiers in the Mullaitivvu garrison. The Special Forces were airlifted into Alampil, an area close to the Mullaitivvu base. This effectively forced the Tigers to fight on two fronts.

But they managed to hold off the reinforcements and concentrated on attacking the central camp. By evening, the Tigers had overrun the Mullaitivvu camp.

Now the battle shifted to the Alampil area where the reinforcements had landed. The troops were surrounded by the Tigers Special Forces units. The Tigers were now unstoppable. Every attempt by the Sri Lankan Army to land more reinforcements was being repulsed.

The Naval forces on either side were also engaged in fierce fighting. Nearly, 24 hours after the first attack on the Mullaitivvu camp, a Sri Lankan naval craft, the *'Ranaviru'* which arrived to establish a supply line, was attacked by Sea Tigers off the Mullaitivvu coast. The vessel was sunk along with its entire 40-man crew.

In desperation, the Sri Lankans pressed the Air Force into the battle, employing the Israeli made Kfir and Argentinean Puccara aircraft to bomb the LTTE positions, but to no avail. Realizing the futility of continuing the battle, the remaining troops who had arrived as reinforcements, withdrew to safer positions.

The Sri Lankan Army lost 1200 soldiers, including at least 20 senior officers, in the audacious attack by the LTTE. The scars of the loss were to remain on the Army's collective psyche for years. Although the LTTE too lost over 400 hardcore fighters, Prabhakaran once again showed that there was no one better than him in planning and executing counter attacks when the Tigers' appeared to be cornered.

The loss of Mullaitivvu was a crippling blow to the seemingly resurgent Sri Lankan Army. It lost not only 1200 soldiers but also had the mortification to see the entire stock of 120 mm artillery stored in the Mullaitivvu camp, fall in the Tigers' hand. This armory in the hands of the LTTE was to prove lethal in subsequent battles.

More importantly, by seizing Mullativvu from the Sri Lankan Army, Prabhakaran had acquired 'depth' for his forces. Now the Sea Tigers, an important element in the LTTE's game plan, had a free run of the Mullaitivvu coast. From then on, most of the LTTE's critical arms and essentials would come through the north eastern coast.

The Sri Lankan Army was aware of the new situation so it planned a bigger military campaign in May 1997 called 'Operation Jayasikiru.' Its aim was simple: regain the LTTE-held Wanni and Mullaitivvu areas and subsequently open a land route through Wanni and Killinochchi districts to link up with the Jaffna Peninsula.

The Sri Lankan Army's most elite Divisions and Brigades were involved in this Operation. Although LTTE lost over 3,000 fighters in the two years of Operation Jayasikiru, it remained firmly entrenched in the Wanni area. However two years after it had launched Operation Jayasikiru, the Army abandoned the campaign without achieving its original objective.

As the fighting raged on in the north, the LTTE struck a telling blow in Colombo.

A powerful blast almost killed President Chandrika Kumaratunga in December 1999. She escaped with the loss of one eye, but the Tigers had once again demonstrated that it could strike in Sri Lanka, anywhere, anytime.

A nervous Kumaratunga, who barely scraped through an election at the end of 1999, perhaps because she had escaped an assassination attempt, had now lost the heart for a battle with the LTTE. Confused political signals led to half-hearted attempts by the military to take back Mullaitivvu and rest of the areas in Wanni.

The LTTE was of course not going to let the Army rest. It hit back and hit back hard in 2000.

An LTTE offensive nicknamed 'Operation Unceasing Waves 3' was so swift, so unconventional and so daring in its execution that the Sri Lankan army troops simply withered away.

The most important battle in this offensive was for the strategic Elephant Pass.

Elephant Pass is a narrow isthmus that connects the Wanni area with the Jaffna Peninsula.

Both the arterial Jaffna-Kandy road, known as the A-9 Highway, and the railway line to Jaffna run through Elephant Pass. The narrow strip of land is in a sense the gateway to Jaffna.

Till 2000, the Elephant Pass was thought to be an impregnable military complex. The LTTE had tried to overrun the military complex way back in 1991 but had been beaten back. The Tigers had then lost over 1000 cadres. But this time the LTTE was better prepared. It launched a multi-pronged offensive on the pass on April 22, 2000.

After days of intense fighting, the LTTE simply overran the large military complex forcing over 10,000 troops to beat a hasty retreat towards Jaffna and Palaly in the North.

The fighting continued until mid-May for the control of the Jaffna peninsula over 1,000 soldiers died in the fighting. The LTTE lost some 200 cadres.

Elsewhere, as garrison after garrison fell to the LTTE, the Army pulled back south to the Vavuniya town. A large number of Sinhala residents in the vicinity fled the area fearing LTTE attacks on their settlements. But the LTTE stopped short of the town, effectively drawing a boundary north of Vavuniya stretching right up to the Elephant Pass to establish a de facto nation.

Prabhakaran at last was the undisputed Lord and Master of Wanni.

Prabhakaran was now at the top of his game while Colombo was at its weakest despite some very significant military victories in the previous decade.

It is this state of mind that Prabhakaran deigned to accept a Norwegian offer for mediation between the LTTE and the Government of Sri Lanka.

For years, Prabhakaran had yearned to be accepted as the leader of a revolutionary outfit. This was at last an opportunity for him to gain recognition from the international community.

For Prabhakaran it was an important moment.

Left with no alternative Prime Minister Chandrika Kumaratunga reluctantly agreed to the Norwegian offer. But for Colombo, involvement of a third party in peace talks was a bitter pill to swallow. However, peace seemed near.

Five years down the line in 2007 the peace talks were a distant memory in Sri Lanka.

By September 2007, the Sri Lankan Army was poised to undertake its biggest mission ever. Gen. Fonseka had raised two new offensive formations called Task Force I and 57 Division. Task Force I was to launch a foray into the Northern Province from the northwestern flank near the coastal town of Mannar and 57 division was deployed to operate along the Vavuniya-Killinochchi axis.

Task force I was to be used as a highly mobile and lethal force in Gen. Fonseka's quest to decimate the LTTE. But even as the Sri Lankan Army was undertaking the initial probing attacks on the LTTE's forward defence lines along the Mannar-Vavuniya axis, Prabhakaran was plotting to launch an audacious counter-attack that caught the Sri Lankan armed forces on the wrong foot again.

Chapter 7

Target Anuradhapura

Anuradhapura town in central Sri Lanka is the site of one of Buddhism's holiest shrines. Mostly inhabited by Sinhalese, the LTTE had in 1983 masscared over 140 Buddhist pilgrims escalating the ethnic clashes. The town is also home to an important base of the Sri Lankan Air Force.

Headquarters of Sri Lankan Air Force's Training Command is based in the town. But at the start of Eelam War IV, several reconnaissance and surveillance aircraft used by the air force were also based at the Anuradhapura base.

A sophisticated Beechcraft plane fitted with equipment for aerial photography and the collection of electronic and technical intelligence and the unmanned aerial vehicles or drones were all based at Anuradhapura. Instructors from Pakistan, China and Israel, who helped Sri Lanka in a big way during Eelam War IV were frequently based at Anuradhapura.

In October 2007 having suffered a major defeat in the East in the previous six months, the LTTE's stock was rather low. The outfit needed to do something spectacular to restore some of its reputation as the world's deadliest guerilla force.

Prabhakaran therefore planned an attack so audacious that only LTTE's elite black Tigers (suicide cadres) could have executed it.

A pre-dawn combined land and air attack by a 21-member Black Tiger squad on October 22 showed why the LTTE remained a potent force even after the defeat in the East. No other terrorist organization in the world would have been capable of organizing such a raid, which was preceded by painstaking intelligence collection, planning and rehearsal.

The commandos, divided into groups, infiltrated into the air base from two directions and, within 20 minutes, took the security guards by surprise, overwhelmed them, seized their weapons and communication equipment, neutralised radar and an anti-aircraft gun position and then intimated their headquarters that they were in effective control of the air base. Only then the two aircrafts of the LTTE's air wing flew to Anuradhapura and dropped two bombs on the base and flew back safely to their hide-out.

The Black Tigers remained in effective occupation of the base for nearly six hours from 3 a.m.

The suicide squad, which included three women cadres, blew up three helicopters, two fixed-wing aircraft—one of them a trainer—and three unmanned drones. The LTTE commandos also managed to cut off the communication of the air base with the rest of the Air Force. Alarmed at the daring raid, a Sri Lankan Air Force helicopter from nearby Vavuniya base was sent to Anuradhapura to find out what had happened. As it was approaching the air base, the helicopter was shot down by the LTTE commandos manning the anti-aircraft gun in the air base.

With no one to stop them now, the LTTE cadres blew up an ammunition storage depot at the air base and damaged its runway. Army reinforcements were rushed to the airbase but by that time, nine air force personnel inside the base and four in the approaching helicopter were already killed. After three hours of intense combat, the entire suicide squad was also killed. It was an act of unbelievable determination, bravery and precision by the LTTE suicide squad.

Although Sri Lanka tried to play down the attack, once again the LTTE had dealt a huge psychological blow to the armed forces by penetrating a highly-secure base and destroying valuable air force assets.

Commented P K Balachandran of *Hindustan Times*: "The fledgling air arm of the Liberation Tigers of Tamil Eelam (LTTE) comprising two to five single engine, propeller driven Zlin-143s, is up against Sri Lanka's formidable air force comprising MIG-27 and Kfir fighter bombers, K-8 jet trainers, MI-24 helicopter gun ships, Bell-

212s choppers, and Antonov troop and material carriers. And yet, the Lankan Goliath has been unable to tame the Tamil David, who has hit and run with impunity four times since March 26 this year."

The Anuradhapura attack was certainly the biggest setback for the Sri Lankan military after its triumphant march in the East just a couple months before the daring air raid by the LTTE.

A lot of thought and planning went into the attack. A Tamil website www.pathivu.com had uploaded a panel discussion about the Anuradhapura attack on an LTTE-run Television station Tamil National Television. In that programme, S Yogaratnam Yogi, head of the LTTE's History Division recalled that the attack on the air base was Prabhakaran's brainchild and showed his penchant for meticulous planning, high secrecy, hard training and meticulous execution. "The Leader was very keen that the operation should not fail. And towards this end, the planning and training for the attack and its execution were kept a top secret. Very few people even at the top most level knew about it. A lot of work had gone into it from the stage of planning to execution," Yogi said on October 28.

Participating in the same programme, the LTTE's military spokesman, Rasaiah Ilanthirayan alias Marshall, said that the Anuradhpura air base was chosen out of many other Sri Lankan military installations because of its centrality in Sri Lanka's military structure in the North.

The Anuradhapura base was a strategic communications, logistics and command centre, he pointed out. It was a training, medical and repatriation centre, and a springboard for campaigns in the Wanni and the northern parts of the Eastern province. It was from here that the SLAF was observing the goings-on in the LTTE-controlled areas of the Wanni and the deep sea through aerial surveillance by manned and unmanned aircraft, he explained.

In the past this kind of an attack would have been a morale-shattering blow for the forces but in 2007, the tenor and character of the higher military leadership in Sri Lanka was completely different. All the three chiefs and the defence secretary were not willing to be cowed down by these obvious reverses. Instead stopping or slowing down operations, they decided to strike back decisively.

Perhaps for the first time in the history of Eelam Wars, the Sri Lankan state hit back in a coordinated strike at the very heart of the LTTE's administrative headquarters in Killinochchi.

Based on accurate and real time intelligence provided by military intelligence, Sr Lankan Air Force jets launched a precision strike at the headquarters of LTTE's Peace Secretariat and killed SP Tamilselvan, head of the outfit's political division on November 3, less than a fortnight after the Anuradhapura attacks by the Tamil Tigers. Five others were killed in the early morning bombing along with Tamilselvan, regarded as No. 2 in the LTTE at the time. The chief of Strategic Communication Division of the LTTE, Anupumani alias Alex, was among the other five LTTE members killed in the incident, the government said.

Tamilselvan had escaped death twice with injuries during two operations launched by the troops in October 1993 and had turned partly disable due to those injuries. He was an active military cadre of the LTTE since 1985.

With Prabhakaran rarely seen publicly in recent years, Tamilselvan had become the rebels' link to the outside world.

He participated in all rounds of peace talks held after the signing of the Ceasefire Agreement on February 22, 2002 in Thailand, Norway, Germany and Japan. Tamilselvan also presided over the LTTE conference in Paris on August 23, 2003.

In 2005, Tamilselvan headed a LTTE delegation to Europe and toured Norway, Sweden, Germany, Belgium, Switzerland, Austria, Finland, Italy, Netherlands, South Africa and Ireland.

Tamilselvan also participated in the Geneva talks between the Government and the LTTE held from February 22 to 23, 2006 and again from October 28 and 29, 2006 in Geneva. His rising stature in the LTTE hierarchy was evident from the fact that Tamilselvan would summon veteran politicians and Tamil National Alliance MPs to Killinochchi and issue directives.

Tamilselvan had become the LTTE's public face mainly because he gave interviews to all visiting media persons in Killinochchi. Although not very fluent in speaking English, Tamilselvan understood every word of the language. He often spoke through his interpreter George, a former postmaster, who later surrendered to the Sri Lankan Army in the final phase of the operations in May 2009.

The importance and stature of Tamilselvan in the LTTE was acknowledged by Prabhakaran himself, who accorded him with the highest military rank of 'brigadier'. In Prabhakaran's own words, Tamilselvan's death was an "unparalleled loss" for the Tigers.

Defence Secretary Gotabaya Rajapaksa, commenting on Tamilselvan's killing said: "This is just a message that we know where their leaders are. I know the locations of all the leaders, that if we want we can take them one by one, so they must change their hideouts. When the time comes only, we take them one by one."

The LTTE responded very quickly to this death and asked its police chief, B. Nadesan, to hold additional charge as political wing leader. But Nadesan's experience as a political spokesman was nowhere near that of Tamilselvan.

Publicly though, the LTTE expressed its unhappiness with the Norwegian mediators for not officially reacting to Tamilselvan's killing. The LTTE's 'serious concern' was conveyed to Maj Gen Lars Johan Solvberg, the head of the Scandinavian-staffed Sri Lanka Monitoring Mission (SLMM) by the new head of the political division, Nadesan nearly a week after the killing.

The Tamilnet website reported that Nadesan had asked Solvberg to tell the Norwegian government that the Tigers regretted its silence.

The former Norwegian chief negotiator, Erik Solheim, had also condoled Tamilselvan's death. But the Norwegian government, like other governments, had made no comment.

Tamilselvan's death expectedly evoked major reactions in Tamil Nadu too. Leaders of major political parties in Tamil Nadu, including the ruling DMK party, paid tribute to Tamilselvan. Tamil Nadu Chief Minister M. Karunanidhi, in fact penned a poem as a tribute to the LTTE leader. Karunanidhi was trying to achieve two aims in one go: reiterate his solidarity with the Tamils of Sri Lanka and two, send a subtle warning to New Delhi that he wasn't too happy with the ruling United Progressive alliance (UPA) government's "hands off" policy towards Sri Lanka's war effort.

This was not the first time that Karunanidhi was playing politics with the Sri Lankan issue. In 1990, when the IPKF was returning home, beaten and battered through its three-year sojourn in Sri Lanka, Karunanidhi as chief minister had refused to attend the reception for the troops when they landed in Madras.

Karunanidhi was not alone in whipping up the sentiments in Tamil Nadu. Dr Ramadoss, leader of Paattali Makkal Katchi (PMK) which was part of the ruling coalition, described Tamilselvan's killing as an "attack against peace and human rights." In a statement designed to incite people, he said: "Through the heinous assassination of Tamilselvan, the Sri Lankan government has clearly demonstrated its non-commitment to peace and its intention of wiping out the Tamil race from the island." Ramadoss said the people of Tamil Nadu—who share the ethnicity, language and culture with Sri Lankan Tamils—should no longer be spectators to the suffering of Eelam Tamils.

Even as political temperatures rose in Tamil Nadu, the Sri Lankan Army raised the stakes in the conflict by relaunching the Wanni operations, beginning what turned out to be the longest and bloodiest phase of Eelam War IV.

Chapter 8
Raiding Wanni

The previous three wars between the Sri Lankan forces and the LTTE were fought between a lumbering Sri Lankan Army, which marched in classical battle strategy, more interested in capturing territory than killing the enemy. A far more nimble and highly mobile Tamil Tigers often attacked a static army and vanished into the jungle as quickly as they came, inflicting heavy damage in the process.

As Army Commander, Gen. Sarath Fonseka had decided to turn this strategy on its head. "We were far too slow to take on the smaller and quicker terrorists teams in the past. So I decided to form the 8-man teams, who were independent, mobile and lethal," Fonseka told me. These teams would often go behind the enemy lines, strike at the heart of LTTE bases, cut off or destroy the LTTE's supply lines and return to base. The Special Forces teams had high success rate in the East, although many soldiers did die in the fierce encounters that took place, often deep in the jungles of the East.

In November 2007, as the Army was poised to start its operations in Wanni, Fonseka and his field commanders decided to add another surprise element to the tested strategy. Instead of concentrating on just one front, the Army decided to launch simultaneous attacks all across the nearly 120 km long LTTE Forward Defence Line or FDL stretching from Mannar in the west to Weli Oya in the east and running through Vavuniya in between.

The other Forward Defence Line (FDL) in the Jaffna theatre stretched for about 12 km on the neck of the Jaffna peninsula. In the Jaffna theatre, troops of 53 and 55 Divisions maintained active defence at three main frontiers—Muhamalai, Kilaly and Nagarkovil.

The forward deployed forces in this theatre acted as the main defensive barricade against any LTTE attack coming from Wanni.

Task Force I which later became 58 Division was operating in North Mannar. The 57 Division was given the task of raiding the FDL in the Vavuniya sector and the 59 Division was asked to start operating at Weli Oya. Simultaneously, two elite divisions—53 and 55—based in the Jaffna peninsula at Jaffna and Kilali respectively, also launched operations against the LTTE's northern defence line.

The concurrent opening of five different fronts was a complete surprise to the LTTE.

In the past, Prabhakaran and his commanders had successfully taken on the Sri Lankan Army because the Army tactics were predictable. The Army would often concentrate at one place and start its operations. This used to make the LTTE's task much easier. Once the Tigers knew where the Army was concentrated at they used to bring in maximum firepower and attack ferociously. The intensity of the attack backed with mortar and artillery firepower used to spread panic in the Army ranks often resulting in the Army either retreating or conceding defeat.

But this army was different. Its leadership was willing to take risks and employ unconventional tactics.

Aware that the LTTE had built up not one but two defence lines all along the Wanni and the Northern front, the Army decided to concentrate on capturing the lines one by one. These defence lines comprised of ditch-cum-bunds running miles on end, backed by heavily fortified bunkers at periodic intervals. I had an opportunity to look at some of these defensive structures in Killinochchi and Mullaitivvu during my frequent visits to the frontlines in 2008 and 2009. Each of these earthen bunds were nearly eight feet in height. The ditches, right in front of these bunds, would often be four to five feet deep. The bunkers were constructed behind the earthen bunds.

These defensive measures, the LTTE had reckoned, would hold off the Sri Lankan Army and tire the troops in prolonged battles. In itself, these rows upon rows of ditch-cum-bunds were an excellent idea when the Sri Lankan Army used to employ the age-old tactics of advancing in a column or company strength and capturing territory. Unfortunately for the LTTE, the Army was no longer using those known tactics.

Instead, the army decided to capture areas behind the enemy lines north of Madhu jungles. This made the hitherto impregnable places redundant, as the LTTE's supplies and reinforcements were automatically cut off, forcing the Tigers to withdraw its beleaguered cadres.

The first offensive was launched in the third week of September 2007 by the 58 Division, commanded by the burly Brig. Shavindra Silva. The division first started operating south of the Mannar area, near a place called Giant Tank. The 581 Brigade, one of the three brigades under the 58 division took control of the area North West of Giant Tank. It started operating East of Adampan taking control over Uyilankulam-Anathankulam road after advancing into Tiger territory through the Uyilankulam road block. The 582 Brigade advanced towards the general area of Adampan from west to east capturing Manthai, Narikulam, Chettukuli and Vannakkuli while the 583 Brigade moved towards Adampan from the Uyilankulam Cross Loading point through Neelachchenai and Palakkuli.

After three months of fierce fighting along this area, the 58 division took control of nearly 50 square kilometres in the Mannar Rice Bowl. The terrain here—plain paddy fields stretching miles on end—favored the army since it could employ tanks and armored personnel carriers from the recently raised mechanized infantry division.

Sri Lanka's Mechanized Infantry Division, the latest addition to the force comprises a mix of regular infantry formations and heavy tanks, armored personnel carriers (APC) and infantry fighting vehicles (IFV) from the fledgling Armored Corps. The division was strengthened with the induction of over 100 new Chinese built APCs in 2007.

The mechanized infantry division was tasked to invade LTTE territory utilizing brute force provided by the armored vehicles and then deploy infantry troops to consolidate the gains. The Mechanized

Infantry Division, commanded by Colonel Ralf Nugera, consists of three specially trained regiments and has a wide variety of armored vehicles including BTR-80A, BMP-2 and WZ551 under its wing.

Later briefing us, the visiting media, Brig. Shavindra Silva revealed the Army's initial strategy. He said: "Our aim was to inflict maximum casualties on the LTTE in the open, plain fields of the Mannar rice bowl. By launching an operation in the far west, we forced the LTTE to send its reinforcements away from its firm bases deep inside the Wanni jungles. They walked straight into our trap. Since we had commando teams operating behind their lines, we managed to cut off their logistics supply chain and inflict maximum casualties in this area."

By the end of January 2008, intercepted LTTE radio transmissions revealed that the Tigers had lost over 600 cadres in just three months of fighting in the west of Mannar Rice Bowl. But the progress was extremely slow.

If the 58 division was slowly advancing along the A-32 Highway on Sri Lanka's west coast, the 57 Division was making equally slow progress in the middle sector along the FDL around the area north of Vavuniya town. In 2007, the 57 Division was under the command of Brigadier Jagath Dias, later to become a major general and then appointed as an envoy to Germany.

This division had started deep penetration strikes in early 2007 even as the Army was engaged in the Eastern Province operations. By December that year, the 57 Division had managed to capture strategic locations in Vavuniya /Killinochchi border. After intense battles along a 45 km long front extending from Kannaiadi to Navi in the North of the A-36 Mannar-Vavuniya road, the 57 division took firm control of over 200 sq km area.

Three brigades under this division—571, 572 and 573—faced fierce resistance from the LTTE in the first three to four months of 2007 but after the capture of the first bunker line in May, the troops had a relatively easier passage northwards.

By December 2007, troops advancing on the Madhu road were operating just three kilometres away from the Madhu area after consolidating their positions in the Thampanai and Periyathampanai villages. It was after a month long battle that the troops were able to capture Thampanai village which was bobby-trapped by the LTTE.

The next target was to neutralize the artillery guns located in the famous Madhu Church complex. After months of continuous battles, the LTTE was beginning to feel the shortage of manpower. The multi-front offensive launched by the army was forcing the LTTE to spread its cadre thin. The lack of numbers was beginning to take a toll on the LTTE resistance.

Like in Mannar in the West, the strategy to lure more and more LTTE cadres into the plains area along the original FDL in Vavuniya was paying huge dividends to the Army. By trapping and killing the Tigers in large numbers close to the FDL, the Army was able to minimize its own casualties and also stay close to its logistics supply bases.

As 2007 came to a close, the 57 division calculated that it had managed to kill some 1,322 Tiger cadres in the Vavuniya battle front alone. By the Army's own calculations, in 2007, the ratio of soldiers and LTTE cadres killed was 1:5, that is for every soldier killed five LTTE fighters were eliminated.

The third front was opened by the 59 division. Thrown into the battle in November 2007, it started operating in the eastern sector of Weli Oya, east of the strategic A-9 Highway. Three brigades—591, 592 and 593—under this division, headed by Brig. Nandan Uduwwatte had started operating along a 10km wide front around Kokkuthuduvai to Ethavetunuvewa. Troops had started probing the FDL at different points heading north and capturing capturing vital Tiger locations in the Weli Oya sector.

The Army's advance from Weli Oya had a potential to threaten the LTTE's military and logistics bases in the jungles of Mullaitivvu. Even the LTTE's main gun positions would have come within the range of the Sri Lankan artillery once troops moved another 10km deeper into the LTTE territory.

As in other sectors, the troops' forward movement was however extremely slow since the Tigers had a larger presence and better defences along this frontline.

LTTE was not sitting idle though.

Realizing the importance of holding the southern FDL firm, Prabhakaran sent his seniormost women's military wing cadre Vidusha to strengthen the Vavuniya LTTE FDL. A large number of female cadres were also sent as reinforcements in the Vavuniya FDL area but the Army was now unstoppable. In desperation, Prabhakaran, decided to deploy men from the Charles Anthony Brigade, considered to be a reserve force. Named after his elder son, Charles Anthony, members of this force were rarely used for normal operations. But the rapid advance of the Army was now forcing Prabhakaran to bring his reserves into play.

It was January 2008.

After nearly 18 months of an undeclared war, Mahinda Rajapaksa officially decided to withdraw from the 2002 Ceasefire Agreement brokered by Norway.

It is worth recalling that this was the third time since 1983 that truce between the two sides was giving way to an all out war.

The first official ceasefire between LTTE and Sri Lankan government was signed way back in 1987, following Jayewardene-Rajiv Gandhi Indo-Sri Lanka accord.

However this lasted less than four months. In October 1987, the Sri Lanka Navy arrested 17 Sea Tigers who were transporting arms using a large vessel from India to Point Pedro in Sri Lanka. Repeated LTTE requests to release the prisoners were turned down by then Defense Minister Lalith Athulathmudali. Despite desperate attempts by the commanders of the Indian Peace Keeping Force and the Indian High Commissioner JN Dixit to resolve the issue, Athulathmudali remained adamant.

The issue reached its climax when 12 of the arrested LTTE cadres committed suicide by consuming cyanide while they were being transported to a prison in Colombo. The LTTE retaliated by torturing and killing 8 Sri Lanka Army soldiers who were under its captivity.

Mutilated bodies of the slain soldiers were publicly displayed in the city of Jaffna. This incident marked the end of that ceasefire.

The next ceasefire agreement was signed between the government and LTTE in 1990 when Prabhakaran, in a tactical move to oust the IPKF from the island, had joined hands with the Ranasinghe Premadasa government. A seemingly triumphant Premadasa had brought LTTE representatives to Colombo in Sri Lankan Air Force helicopters for peace talks. Again peace did not last long. LTTE officially pulled out of the truce on 11 June 1990, alleging that a group of Sri Lankan soldiers had assaulted a tailor (who was also a member of the LTTE) in the eastern town of Batticaloa. Immediately after their withdrawal from the ceasefire, LTTE fighters under Karuna Amman (who is now a minister in the Mahinda Rajapaksa government) launched multiple raids on police posts in Batticaloa, massacring over 600 policemen.

There was a brief lull in the fighting in 1994 when President Chandrika Kumaratunga invited the LTTE for peace talks shortly after her victory in the presidential election. Several rounds of peace talks were held but progress in devising a solution that could bring peace to Sri Lanka was extremely slow. Even as the talks were on, on 15th April that year the LTTE launched dual suicide attacks on Sri Lanka Navy warships *SLNS Sooraya* and *SLNS Ranasuru* anchored in Trincomalee harbor. Both the ships were critically damaged in the incident. Some of the conflicts bloodiest battles followed this breakdown in talks.

War raged on for seven years until another peace deal, this time brokered by Norway was signed in February 2002. Although it continued to hold on paper, tension between the two parties had been high since late 2002. The gloves were off in April 2006, when a women suicide bomber tried to kill Army Commander Lt. Gen. Sarath Fonseka within the Army Headquarters premises. The liberation of the Eastern Province in July 2007 and the subsequent Army assault on the LTTE's Wanni stronghold had all but put the ceasefire on the backburner.

On 16 January 2008, Colombo officially withdrew from the 2002 Ceasefire Agreement but Eelam War IV had been on for more than 18 months.

The final battle for Wanni was about to commence. It would ultimately end on May 19, 2009 with Prabhakaran's death.

In January 2008 Army Commander Gen. Sarath Fonseka was neither focused on capturing Prabhakaran nor in attacking Killinochchi, the LTTE's administrative headquarters.

His immediate objective was to recapture the A-32 Highway connecting Mannar-Pooneryn-Paranthan axis on Sri Lankan's west coast. In a complete reversal of the strategies adopted by the Army in the previous three wars, Fonseka had decided to open the Western flank in the Wanni battlefield instead of concentrating on the A-9 Highway that connects Kandy and Jaffna and runs parallel to the eastern coast.

The task to recapture the entire A-32 was entrusted to the 58 Division, which comprised elements of Special Forces besides the traditional infantry units. Having captured the key areas of Madhu Church end of December 2007, 58 Division was making swift progress along the western coast.

Its first big target after Sri Lanka officially withdrew from the ceasefire was Adampan, a small but strategically important town on the north-western coast. But success was slow in coming. The LTTE was putting up a fierce fight. It took the 58 division nearly five months to successfully penetrate the heavy security ring thrown around the Adampan area by the LTTE. But once Adampan was secured on 8 May, in another month's time the entire Mannar Rice Bowl, a plain area of about 120 sq km known for its paddy cultivation was totally under the army's control.

It had taken the 58 Division nearly eight months to push the original Forward Defence Line of the LTTE northwards. Control of the Mannar Rice Bowl area however gave the Army a vital springboard to launch a major attack on LTTE's most important military assest in the north-west: the Sea Tiger base of Vidattaltivu.

The port town of Vidattaltivu on Sri Lanka's northwest coast had been a base for the Tamil Tigers' small boat navy and was an important entry point for arms and other supplies smuggled in by the rebels, mostly from India across the Palk Strait.

Once the troops advanced further northward they found an earth bund similar to the one inside the 'Rice Bowl' area from Pappamoddai to Parappakadattan. The earth bund ran from South of Vidattalthivu up to Piramanayankulam tank some 10 kilometres east of Vidattaltivu. The LTTE had employed some of its best fighters to defend Vidattaltivu.

The troops were equal to the task. Vidattaltivu fell by 16th July.

I remember Brig. Shavindra Silva briefing us about the battle for Vidattaltivu and the time his Division took to beat the Tigers there. "We decided to get the maximum attrition here. We managed to kill over 100 LTTE cadres," he told visiting journalists months after the operation in recounting his formation's successes.

Further success was to come just four days later with the fall of Illuppakkadavai, 10km north of Vidattaltivu. This rapid advance made by the Army troops was in keeping with Fonseka's aim of securing maximum kills and not being bothered too much about capturing territory. In the past, the Sri Lankan Army used to often slow down after a major victory, allowing the LTTE to regroup.

The LTTE was now under tremendous pressure. Although it had managed to pull out nearly 200 cadres before the Vidattaltivu base fell, it was fast losing its logistics bases.

With the fall of Vidattaltivu and Illuppakkadavai, LTTE's maneuvering space to switch troops from east to west and ability to coordinate operations on more than one front was considerably reduced. But Brig. Shavindra Silva had one more important task on hand before he could think of marching onto Pooneryn. He needed to capture Nachchikuda, the LTTE base located 17 km further to the north. Nachchikuda along with Vidattaltivu and Illuppakkadavai were important operational areas for the Sea Tigers since hundreds of Indian fishing boats operating in the vicinity used to hamper Sri Lankan Navy's operations against the Sea Tigers.

This setback was not the only major reversal in the LTTE's fortunes in the summer of 2008.

In May, the Tigers lost one of its most experienced and courageous field commanders. 'Colonel' Balraj, in-charge of LTTE's defences in Wanni had been under increasing pressure over the previous months after the Army had stepped up its offensive along multiple fronts. In absence of adequate number of experienced field commanders, Balraj was forced to direct and control operations on a wide front stretching from Mannar in the West to Weli Oya in the East. He was under pressure to demonstrate the once formidable strength of the LTTE in this sector, but successes came only in small measures.

The strain took its toll and Balraj, who had already undergone treatment for a cardiac condition during the ceasefire, died of a massive heart attack in May 2008. Balraj, the first commander of the elite Charles Anthony infantry unit, considered the first semi-conventional fighting force of the Tigers had earned his military reputation by wresting the Elephant Pass from the Sri Lankan Army in 2000.

But that was eight years ago. Since then, the Sri Lankan Army had become much more effective whereas the Tigers had lost many of its fighting cadres and leaders' like Balraj were slowed down considerably by age and time.

And yet, as July ended, Eelam War IV seemed to be entering a messy and bloody phase.

During the previous two weeks, in the Mannar sector the 58 Division troops progressed up to Mulankavil on A-32 road to Pooneryn, increasing the threat to LTTE defences for Pooneryn and Killinochchi.

In the Weli Oya sector although the 59 Division managed to capture Andankulam base, its progress into the Tiger heartland north and west of Mullaitivvu was extremely slow since the thick jungles and strong LTTE defences here were not easy to overcome. But the Army persisted and kept the operations going.

Between September 2007 and July 2008, Fonseka demonstrated that his strategy to open multiple fronts against the LTTE was successful beyond expectations. This phase of the war amply demonstrated how Sri Lankan Army is now a changed force. It overcame its earlier weaknesses on three difficult aspects—higher coordination of war involving multiple formations, effective use of commandos in tandem with conventional operations, and retaining military initiative at all times. Nearly 5,500 LTTE fighters were killed in this phase, more than justifying the Army Commander's confidence in the troops and formation commanders. The Army too lost over 800 soldiers in this phase.

But from now on, Fonseka's skills as a leader would be severely tested.

As the Army made further inroads deeper into LTTE held territory, the lines of communication were bound to stretch and become vulnerable to LTTE interdiction or even blocks. Fonseka and his commanders had of course anticipated such an eventuality.

As he told me at the end of the war: "One of the many unconventional things that we did in Eelam War IV was not to depend too much on the traditional supply routes. The LTTE expected us to march on, hugging the roads. But my troops were more than willing to abandon the conventional way. They marched through jungles, waded through chest deep water under pouring rain and yet kept going forward. This took the terrorists completely by surprise. They had never seen the Army adopt such tactics. Those were supposed to be the LTTE tactics in many people's eyes. But my commanders and troops showed adaptability and daring in turning the conventional strategies on their head to totally confuse and annihilate the terrorists."

If Fonseka was able to motivate and inspire his soldiers to give more than 100 per cent, Prabhakaran was hampered by several factors. His movements were restricted because the Long Range Reconnaissance Patrols (LRRP) and Deep Penetration Units of the Army were constantly harassing the LTTE leaders by their surprise raids. The Sri Lankan Air Force was also doing its bit in keeping Prabhakaran and his top leaders pinned down in their hideouts. As a result, the young cadres, especially those who were recruited recently, were bereft of any real inspiration. Restricted movement of the leaders also meant that the LTTE fighting units lacked tactical guidance during actual fighting.

The LTTE leadership also bungled both strategically and tactically. Its decision to depend on a strategy described by one expert as "First World War vintage," cost the Tigers heavily.

Col. R. Hariharan, IPKF veteran, wrote in an article: "The (LTTE's) conventional defence strategy appears to be based upon a series of strong points with bunds and ditches stretching for miles between them. The bunds along the expected axes of advance have been constructed to slow down the advancing troops and attack them at selected points when they try to break through the obstacle."

"This is a strategy of the First World War vintage that became obsolete with the advent of increased battlefield mobility, greater depth and density of fire power, and enhanced battlefield reconnaissance capabilities. Unless the bund is protected by fire power and layers of obstacles, modern armies can reduce their effectiveness with no great difficulty."

"In modern conventional warfare the technique has morphed into mobile defence based upon strong points that dominate the gaps between them with hard hitting armor based mobile teams. But the LTTE had neither the required mobility nor fire power to dominate the gaps between the strong points to stop the security forces that had superior mobility, fire power and numbers. So probably it took recourse to constructing miles of bunds between strong points."

In the previous conflicts, the LTTE always had a nasty surprise up its sleeve, whenever it was cornered. But in Eelam War IV, it had failed to launch a counter-strike that would turn the tide or at least make the Army think twice. On the contrary, all military weaknesses of an insurgent group trying to fight a conventional war were showing up in LTTE's operations. LTTE fighters were good at tackling small tactical attacks but they clearly lacked the firepower or capability to take on a large conventional army which outnumbered the Tigers one is to eight if not one is to ten.

Prabhakaran had also miscalculated on several fronts. He had underestimated the loss of 'Col' Karuna and his 6,000-odd followers from the East and not taken into account the new resolve and qualitative improvement of the armed forces.

'Col' Karuna, who had spent some months in a UK jail for possession of a forged visa, had returned to Sri Lanka and joined the ruling SLFP and was named Minister for reconciliation and National Integration by President Rajapaksa in 2008.

During a long interview with me in his heavily fortified residence in Colombo a month before Eelam War IV ended, Karuna gave me a fairly accurate assessement of why the LTTE was no longer able to turn the tide against the Sri Lankan Armed Forces. He said: "The LTTE had lost its capacity to launch 'Operation Ceaseless Waves' kind of attacks since the defection of the Eastern faction under me. Moreover, Prabhakaran had not allowed new commanders to emerge. And people like Balraj, Swarnam, Soosai, Jeyam and Bhanu were not getting any younger. There was too much pressure on these old-timers which showed up in the untimely death of Balraj due to cardiac arrest. But more than anything else, Prabhakaran's inability to read the changed situation, cost him dearly."

What Karuna did not mention was the fact that Prabhakaran had also made a major strategic error in herding a large number of civilians together as the LTTE retreated deeper into the Wanni heartland. The presence of over 100,000 civilians—old, young, men and women and thousands of children—was to play a critical role in the war over the next eight months.

Till July-August 2008, the army had managed to avoid entanglement with civilian population by by-passing small towns or spending minimal time in populated areas. But as the battle for Wanni looked poised to intensify, the Army was forced to factor in the 'non-military,' aspect of Eelam War IV since areas around Pooneryn, Mankulam and Killinochchi had a well-settled civilian inhabitation.

The moment troops started advancing deeper into the Wanni areas, reports of civilians getting killed and injured in artillery shelling and air force bombing started emanating from the LTTE side.

On 13th August, the LTTE peace secretariat website claimed that troops had shelled a hospital in Mullaitivvu, a charge the Army and the Air force immediately refuted.

Gen. Fonseka was quoted in local media reports saying the LTTE was creating a human shield in Wanni and shelling those areas to tarnish the Security Forces' image.

"The LTTE is holding these civilians as a human shield. We have never fired artillery in to the civilian populated areas since these areas are located some 15 kilometres away from the Forward Defence Lines," the Army Commander told the Daily News.

"The LTTE is shelling these areas and trying to put the blame on us," the Commander added.

The Army Commander said that the Government had already sent a message to the people entrapped in Wanni to arrive in Government controlled areas. "The LTTE is holding them forcibly without allowing them to leave those areas. If they come to our side we are ready to receive them in Vavuniya providing them food and shelter."

Gen. Fonseka said that around 200,000 people were living in Killinochchi and Mullaittivvu districts along with 30,000 displaced civilians. The LTTE was keeping them forcibly and providing military training for deployment in the FDLs, he charged.

As we will see in the subsequent chapter, the fate of these civilians became a major bone of contention between the Sri Lankan government and the international community in the last five months of Eelam War IV.

Having captured Vidattaltivu and Nachchikuuda, Fonseka gave orders to go for the next big strategic target—Pooneryn.

A coordinated army-navy offensive against Pooneryn was planned for early September. Control of Pooneryn was vital to Fonseka's plan to open a second lifeline to Jaffna through A32 road reducing the importance of A-9 Highway.

There was another reason for the Sri Lankan Army to plan the attack on Pooneryn with meticulous care.

Nearly 15 years ago, in November 1993, Pooneryn was the scene of a major debacle faced by the Army at the hands of the rampaging LTTE. Over 600 officers and soldiers had been massacred by the

LTTE in that surprise attack. The nation was outraged. The confidence of the armed forces was its lowest following that defeat.

Pooneryn is located at the southern shore of the Jaffna lagoon and whoever control led the area had a quick alternate access to the peninsula when the main road, the A-9 Highway was not open. In 1993, the Army camp at Pooneryn was intended to prevent the Tigers from using the lagoon to supply the peninsula. But the Tigers wanted to control the area.

Describing the attack, John Rettie of the London-based based *Guardian* newspaper said on 12 November, 1993: "The attack began before daybreak on 11 November when heavily armed Tigers fell upon the base, raking the skies with anti aircraft fire to prevent the use of helicopter gunships. When dawn broke, they had overrun large parts of the base. Some army units held out in bunkers along the sandy shore. Several hundred men were reported to have been evacuated. The Tigers captured several naval gunboats, heavy mortars and two tanks though one was later destroyed in an air attack—and large quantities of other arms and ammunition."

Prime Minister Ranil Wickremasinghe, speaking about the attack in the Parliament said in late November 1993: "On November 11, around 0200 hours, the LTTE launched a massive attack from land and the lagoon simultaneously engaging the Nagathevanthurai naval base and the army defence lines in Pooneryn. It is now believed that prior to the attack, the LTTE had managed to infiltrate a group through the Forward Defence Lines (FDLs), who had overrun the gun positions and the armor positions. As a result of the attack, the Nagathevanthurai naval base was overrun and all crafts were destroyed or taken over by the LTTE."

After an uproar in the Parliament, the then Army Commander appointed a Court of Enquiry to establish what caused the debacle. Quoting from the enquiry report, *Sunday Island,* Sri Lanka's influential newspaper, reported on 16 January 1994. "The report states that the (Pooneryn) attack had begun at 1.30 a.m. on the 11th of November and within around 15 minutes the whole command structure had broken down and there were no platoons, companies or battalions. There were only men and officers running around in confusion. The troops did not know who was friend or foe. There was no way of identifying anyone in the dark as no password system had been put in place. The LTTE had used white arm bands to identify themselves and they also used green torchlights and yellow flags during daytime. By 6 a.m. on the 11th, the forward defence lines had fallen..."

"The Court was of the view that around 400 LTTE infiltrators would have entered the camp through undefended lines before the attack. The report notes that Tamil villagers who were living as refugees within the defence lines had also provided a base for infiltrators ... the T55 battle tanks were the first to fall into the hands of the enemy. The tanks had been abandoned without offering any resistance. The tank troops had lost even their personal weapons in the melee with a tank troop leader losing even his radio set. The Court of Inquiry found that with the first assault, the troops had dispersed in confusion, small informal groups were formed. These broke up into even smaller groups as the attack continued and ultimately it had been every man for himself.

The troops had fought only for survival and a distinct lack of motivation ... and a fear of the enemy was detected. According to the Court of Inquiry, troops which had got detached from command ... had been firing into the night more out of fear than at any target. Thereby ammunition had been exhausted... The day immediately after the attack the LTTE went about the defences of Pooneryn camp attending to their casualties.... In his statement to the Court of Inquiry, Maj. General Daluwatte had charged that fire battalion had been withdrawn from Pooneryn and sent to the East to boost the Eastern Commander. According to sources this decision was made by the Secretary of Defence in the preparation made for holding elections in the East ... Radio contact broke down during the attack due to lack of serviceable batteries."

It was an unmitigated disaster and showed up the Army in extremely poor light. The top generals had been guilty of poor leadership and bad planning. Wrote another commentator: "A string of stunning military victories, capture of tanks and artillery from Sri

Lankan army have made the LTTE a phantom force, which the Sri Lankan security forces now fear."

The spectacular capture of Pooneryn in 1993 gave the LTTE a military foothold that the outfit exploited to the hilt. Strategically, Pooneryn was critically important for the LTTE as it was from here (Kalmunai Point) that it directed the long range 130mm artillery fire which threatened military bases on the Jaffna peninsula including the Pallali airfield.

It was against this backdrop that Fonseka handpicked the 58 Division, led by their daring commander, Brig. Shavindra Silva to launch an assault on Pooneryn. The 58 Division had been Fonseka's spearhead ever since he ordered the commencement of the Wanni operations in September 2007. Recalled Brigadier, now a Major General, Shavindra Silva: "We in 58 Division commenced our operation at a time when the LTTE was operating along the Vavuniya-Mannar road threatening military vehicles and military convoys. Many of the troops going on leave and reporting back to duty and other military vehicles frequently came under LTTE attacks."

"The Division was initially formed with the Task Force -I with a strength of two Brigades concentrated on liberating Mannar 'Rice Bowl.' We killed more than 2000 Tiger cadres in Operation 'Rice Bowl' which took nearly 10 months for the 58 Division to accomplish under bad weather conditions."

But the 58 Division did not stop after liberating the Rice Bowl on 29th June. From then on in fact, the Division made rapid progress overrunning the Viddathaltivu sea base and capturing Illuppakadavai, one of the important townships in the North of Mannar on the Mannar-Pooneryn A-32 Road. By August 7, troops reached Vellankulam, the last township in the Mannar District, where LTTE had many of its offices, Police stations and political organizations, completely liberating the Mannar District from the LTTE's control.

This relentless march by the 58 Division was unprecedented. The troops just did not rest as the LTTE would have expected. Instead it went on to capture Vellankulam in the next five days and entered the

Killinochchi district to overun Mullankavil, considered the second most important township in the District. It was August 13, 2008.

After the briefing I could not resist asking Brigadier, now Major General, Shavindra Silva how he managed to keep the momentum going.

His answer was simple: "We were given a particular task and there was no way we as ground commanders and soldiers were going to let down our Army Commander." Clearly, Fonseka had instilled a fierce sense of pride among the soldiers and motivated them to accomplish seemingly impossible tasks. So, despite inclement weather and hostile terrain, Shavindra Silva was able to maintain the momentum.

Their immediate target on way to Pooneryn was a 30-km long bund stretching from Nachchikuda to Akkarayankulam in the Mulankavil area. After breaching the LTTE earth bund from Karamabakulam, troops advanced immediately to the North and took control of 13-km stretch North of Nachchikuda from an area called Madam on the A-32 Road.

Having captured Madam, the LTTE expected troops to advance towards Kiranch and Vallaipadu but Shavindra Silva sent the Army teams on a different route surprising the LTTE defenders. The Tigers were however offering fierce resistance all along the route. By October 10, putting two weeks of sunny weather to good use, troops of the 58 Division advanced on a broad front south east of A-32 Mannar-Pooneryn road. They were now just six kilometres short of Pooneryn. The LTTE was of course fighting to the last man at Palayilkulam and Uruthirapuram although it had already withdrawn two of its 130 mm howitzers earlier located at the Kalmunai point deeper in the jungles of Killinochchi.

Even as operations to regain Pooneryn by the 58 Division were on, Fonseka had directed the 57 Division, operating west of the A-9 Highway, to interdict any LTTE reinforcements that would have come to the aid of the Tigers fighting in the Pooneryn area.

On October 6, after two months of intermittent fighting, the 57 Division advancing west of A-9 captured the well sited Akkarayankulam defence complex. The army said it had neutralized the long bund obstacle after fighting a few bitter battles in the area. The Division's progress was slowed down due to strong opposition from the LTTE and also because the area was heavily mined.

By the first week of November, 58 Division was knocking at the gates of Pooneryn. It took the troops another week to overcome a spirited defence of the town by the remaining Tigers. Finally On 15th November, almost 15 years to date when the Army was roundly defeated by the LTTE in this area, troops of the 58 Division seized control of Pooneryn town.

Events had come full circle.

In 1993, the Army had fled the area in ignominy.

In November 2008, the LTTE retreated from Pooneryn, unable to withstand the fierce onslaught by the troops of the 58 Division.

The victory was considered important both strategically and emotionally. No wonder President Mahinda Rajpakasa went on National Television and Radio to announce the recapture of Pooneryn.

"The entire A-32 road and Pooneryn was captured by our security forces," the President said. "On this occasion, I ask Prabhakaran to lay down arms and immediately come for talks." "The best thing he can do for the (Tamil) people in the North is to lay down arms and surrender," the President said in his nationally televised speech.

With the fall of Pooneryn, the military took full control of the north-western seaboard of the island. This finally allowed the military to open a new land route to the Jaffna peninsula, which had so far been supplied only by sea and air routes.

The victory had come at a considerable cost though. At least 8 officers and 48 soldiers were killed and 311 were wounded in the last days of the Pooneryn battle.

That time there was no way to confirm the casuality figures as the military had stopped releasing its own casualty figures in daily bulletins since September 2008.

However, media reports of the time said official figures tabled in Parliament showed 1,269 troops were killed in the first 10 months of 2008. The military claimed killing more than 7,500 Tigers during the same period.

Later I asked Defence Secretary Gotabaya Rajapaksa why casuality figures were being withheld. He said: "The media used the figures to raise doubts among the people about the military campaign. Even when we were winning, distorted media reports interpreting the casualties was demoralizing the troops. So we stopped giving the figures."

The Sri Lankan Army's victory at Pooneryn came just two weeks before Prabhakaran's annual address to his followers. Many were eagerly awaiting the speech. Would Prabhakaran, having lost the Eastern Province and now Mannar followed by fall of Pooneryn, sue for peace? Or would he once again pull a rabbit out of the hat, as he had done a number of times in the past when cornered?

Would his supporters among the Tamil Diaspora and especially in Tamil Nadu launch a political rescue mission? And would President Rajapaksa be able to withstand pressure from the international community, which was bound to increase in the coming weeks as the Sri Lankan forces advanced towards the very heart of LTTE territory?

Chapter 9
The Indian Connection

A Speech, A Plea, and A Hidden Hand

Every year on 27 November, Vellupillai Prabhakaran used to make what he called a Hero's Day speech, often reassuring his supporters that the fight for Tamil Eelam was still on. Given the setbacks suffered by the LTTE in the first 10 months of 2008, Prabhakaran's speech was awaited with much anticipation. Would he appeal to Indian leadership to rescue him? Or would he seek a ceasefire?

The speech was expected to reveal Prabhakaran's mind.

But destiny had other plans for the beleagured leader.

Just when Prabhakaran needed the undivided attention of India, particularly the people of Tamil Nadu, terrorists of the Lashkar-e-Toiba blasted their way into the headlines by attacking India's financial capital Mumbai late on November 26, completely shutting Prabhakaran out of the Indian news media.

Holding the city to ransom for three days the terror story hogged headlines and only few of the Indian print media carried Prabhakaran's speech on the sidelines, while the visual media totally ignored it.

This, at a time when Prabhakaran needed India and more particularly, Tamil Nadu to react to the LTTE's plight. This was the time when he needed India's total attention. This was the time he needed India's support for his armed struggle. This was the time he needed India to lift the ban on the LTTE.

Actually this was the central theme of his otherwise recycled, annual speech in November 2008.

In political terms it meant that whatever little glimmer of hope there was for an Indian intervention to stop the war on terror in Sri Lanka went up in smoke in the flames burning in Mumbai.

His hopes were based on the fact that in the previous six months, there had been a resurgence of political support in Tamil Nadu for the LTTE.

Prabhakaran was once again hoping to manipulate Delhi through Chennai.

Prabhhkaran's Hero's Day speech in 2008—which turned out to be his last—outlined his political strategy: "Notwithstanding the dividing sea, Tamil Nadu, with its perfect understanding of our plight, has taken heart to rise on behalf of our people at this hour of need. This timely intervention has gratified the people of Tamil Eelam and our freedom movement and given us a sense of relief. I wish to express my love and gratitude at this juncture to the people and leaders of Tamil Nadu and the leaders of India for the voice of support and love they have extended. I would cordially request them to raise their voice firmly in favor of our struggle for a Tamil Eelam state, and to take appropriate and positive measures to remove the ban which remains an impediment to an amicable relationship between India and our movement."

And yet, there not a word of regret or remorse in the speech for his own betrayal of India in the past when New Delhi had actively intervened in support of the Tamil cause but only got a bloody nose and unfair criticism from rest of the world. Despite the recent military reversals, Prabhkaran wanted India's help on his own terms. He offered no apology for the role of LTTE in the assassination of Rajiv Gandhi, India's prime minister in 1991.

Instead he called India's past actions as "injurious to the people of Tamil Eelam, as well as to their struggle." Contradicting himself in the latter part of his speech Prabhakaran said he had "great expectations that the Indian super power will take a positive stand on our national question." Probably, he expected further political pressure from Tamil Nadu to influence India. He felt Tamil Nadu "has taken heart to rise on behalf of our people at this hour of need. This timely intervention has gratified the people of Tamil Eelam and our freedom movement and given us a sense of relief."

Col Hariharan analysed the speech in its correct context and asked: "Does he (Prabhakaran) really believe in his call? Or a stray event like the celebration of his birthday by a group of lawyers in the Madras High Court has kindled his high expectations? Prabhakaran is too shrewd for that. All this hype built over Indian support is probably to boost up his constituency among expatriate Tamils and the LTTE cadres battling it out in Wanni under adverse conditions."

"The Great Hero's Day statement only shows that despite his strategic blunders Prabhakaran is yet to introspect and come to term with the dynamics of sub-continental reality. If he wants Indian support he has to change his script drastically. And it has to be on India's terms, not his."

As 2008 drew to a close, Prabhakaran would have looked back and wondered if his mistakes in alienating India would cost him dearly in the coming months.

This was quite a change from a quarter century ago. Then the Tamils in Sri Lanka had looked at India as the savior and so did the LTTE.

Twenty-five years later, India sought to protect Tamil civilians caught in the conflict but New Delhi had clearly told the Sri Lankan government that it considered the LTTE a terrorist organization and therefore would not interfere in Colombo's military campaign.

Prabhakaran's ill-fated decision to order Rajiv Gandhi's assassination in the summer of 1991 was now coming back to haunt him.

In reality, the day a female suicide bomber detonated explosives strapped to her body and killed Rajiv Gandhi in a small Tamil Nadu town named Sriperumbadur, Prabhakaran blew up his chances of ever getting India on his side.

To be fair to him though, New Delhi's policies towards Sri Lanka and LTTE in particular, always oscillated widely between two extremes.

In 1983, after the tragic massacre of innocent Tamils in Colombo, India's then Prime Minister Indira Gandhi had initiated a multi-pronged strategy to deal with the Sri Lankan issue. While she facilitated direct talks between moderate Tamil parties and President JR Jayewardene's government, India's external intelligence agency, the Research and Analysis Wing (RAW) began arming and training nascent Tamil insurgent groups, including the LTTE in an effort to bring these groups under India's direct influence and use them as lever against the Sri Lankan state.

In less than two years after Indira Gandhi's initiative, her son Rajiv, who took over the mantle of Prime Ministership after his mother was assassinated on October 31, 1984 almost reversed the policy. In his eagerness to go down in history as a man who brought peace all round, Rajiv Gandhi initiated several accords in India and one with Sri Lanka. He went against the LTTE, got closer to the Sri Lankan state and pushed for political settlement between the Tamil groups and the government. He even ordered the Indian Navy to assist the Sri Lankan navy in patrolling the Palk Strait and prevent Tamil militants groups from smuggling weapons into Sri Lanka and disallow the rebels to flee to Tamil Nadu.

Rajiv Gandhi's policy however failed to yield the desired dividends. In the process, both the Sinhala-dominated J R Jayewardene government and the Tamil rebels blamed New Delhi for messing up the situation. After a failed round of talks in the Bhutanese capital of Thimphu in 1985, Jayewardene resumed military operations against the rebels particularly the LTTE. The Army operations led to a humanitarian crisis in the Jaffna peninsula in 1987 forcing India to airdrop food packets much against the wishes of the Sri Lankan government.

JR Jayewardene chafed at India's 'military' intervention but had little choice then to fall in line. India's openly biased intervention in favor of the Tamils in Sri Lanka led to the Indo-Sri Lanka Accord of July

29, 1987. Under the accord, the Sri Lankan government agreed to make constitutional changes for devolving powers to the Tamil. In return, the Indian Peacekeeping Force (IPKF), which had arrived on the island's North with great fanfare was supposed to disarm the rebel groups.

But Prabhakaran who had reluctantly acquiesced to the terms of the Accord was not playing ball. Within months of the Accord, the LTTE and IPKF troops were confronting each other. Colombo watched with glee as the two former friends clashed and clashed violently. The IPKF suffered grievously in absence of any clear politico-military objective, lost over 1200 men and returned home bitter and humiliated.

The Indo-Sri Lanka relationship had reached its nadir in 1990.

The LTTE however continued to receive moral and material support in Tamil Nadu until May 21, 1991.

By killing Rajiv Gandhi that day, the outfit lost, in one stroke, its biggest strength: safe sanctuaries in Tamil Nadu. 'Col' Karuna, who was Prabhakaran's trusted commander in the East in 1991, told me in 2009: "The decision to eliminate Rajiv Gandhi was known only to Prabhakaran and Pottu Amman (LTTE's intelligence chief). None of us senior commanders or leaders was taken into confidence. In my view, killing Rajiv Gandhi was the biggest mistake Prabhakaran made in his life."

The outrage over Rajiv Gandhi's assassination forced India to ban the LTTE on May 14, 1992. The event also reversed India's policy of covert support for Tamil militants. Instead of helping the Tamil groups in Sri Lanka, New Delhi ordered a total clampdown on organizations that supported the LTTE.

India in fact went one step forward. It helped Colombo launch a concerted campaign to ban the LTTE worldwide. New Delhi's diplomatic collaboration with Colombo led to major powers like the US and European Union to proscribe the LTTE over the next 15 years.

So between 1991 and 2004, India studiously kept a distance from the ethnic conflict in Sri Lanka although New Delhi pursued a proactive economic and trade relationship with Colombo. India's decided to offer Sri Lanka favorable terms in trade giving New Delhi an increased foothold in Colombo.

Despite the new-found confidence between the two, Mahinda Rajapaksa was not going to be swayed by emotion or fear. As a pragmatist, he realized the importance of keeping New Delhi on his side but he, like many Sri Lankan politicians of his generation, was not about to forget the roughshod treatment meted out by New Delhi in the tumultuous 1980s.

The 1987 Indo-Sri Lanka accord was seen by many in Colombo as Sri Lanka's ultimate humiliation by a big neighbor. That accord was virtually forced on the Sri Lankans. If the Tamils thought New Delhi had sold them out, the Sinhala right chafed at the some of the concession India extracted from Sri Lanka on security matters. *(See annexures)*

Twenty years later, Colombo had not forgotten the terms imposed by India in the aftermath of the 1987 accord.

The then Indian High Commissioner to Colombo, JN Dixit indeed explicitly mentioned in his book *Assignment Colombo* how New Delhi almost arm-twisted Sri Lanka into agreeing to Indian pre-conditions on security aspects. He wrote:

> *... I mentioned to the (Sri Lanka) President that while the Agreement and its Annexure would cover all aspects related to the ethnic problem, India's concerns about India-Sri Lanka bilateral relations and India's political and security concerns had not been taken care of. The President was told that the Prime Minister of India also, would, like him (the President), be taking enormous risks in signing such an Agreement in terms of Indian public opinion and, therefore, there must be some formal understanding between Sri Lanka and India on India's concerns which should be embodied in another Agreement or exchange of letters.*

When Jayewardene asked me to be specific about India's concerns, I said that Sri Lanka should give assurances to India on the following points:

1. Reduction and phasing out of foreign military and intelligence personnel in Sri Lanka from the United Kingdom, Pakistan, Israel, South Africa and so on.

2. Sri Lanka should tilizede its foreign and defence policies and reduce its involvement with USA, Pakistan, China, Israel and South Africa.

3. Sri Lanka should give some assurances to India that its seaports and airports would not be tilized by foreign powers which were antagonistic towards India or which affected India's security interest negatively.

4. Sri Lanka should fulfil the assurances which it gave in 1985 that India would be given an opportunity to maintain the Trincomalee Oil Tank Farms and that Sri Lanka would prevent foreign broadcasting stations like the Voice of America from being tilized for military purposes by countries like the United States, West Germany, etc.

Jayewardene said that these were excessive demands being made at the last moment. He was, however, reminded politely that these concerns of India were specifically mentioned to him between April 29 and May 5, 1985 by Minister Chidambaram. I recalled that I had repeated these concerns and requests to Jayewardene on June 9, 1985. Minister of State Natwar Singh did the same on November 24, and again between December 17 and 19, 1986. I pointed out that India's co-operation with Sri Lanka to solve the ethnic problem was predicated on Sri Lanka giving positive responses on these important concerns of India. The President consulted Minister Gamini Dissanayake and Finance Minister Romaie de Mel over the phone on these points raised by me. He then directed me to proceed immediately to the offices of the two Ministers to discuss details of how this particular issue should be dealt with.

At the end of the meeting with these Ministers, it was agreed that the points raised could be covered by means of a letter which should be carefully drafted. I said I would get a Draft Letter covering these points prepared when I proceeded to Delhi for consultations on the proposed Agreement and bring it back for approval...."

Given such bitter and contentious past, Colombo was always wary of India and Rajapaksa were not about to depend solely on India in their quest to eliminate the LTTE.

INDIA'S HIDDEN HAND

By end of November 2008, the script was no longer in Prabhakaran's hands.

It was being written by the Sri Lankan forces tacitly supported by India and openly assisted by China and Pakistan.

Since December 2005, when Rajapaksa made his first visit to New Delhi less than a month after he took over as President, India was aware of his intention to take the LTTE head on. Although in the initial days he was advised to seek a negotiated settlement with the Tigers, New Delhi saw merit in Rajapaksa's argument that the LTTE was only biding its time to regroup and rearm itself and that war was inevitable sooner than later. And if the LTTE was preparing for a showdown, Rajapaksa did not want to be caught off guard either. His armed forces needed to be ready for any eventuality.

The President therefore sent his brothers Basil and Gotabaya to New Delhi with a shopping list for essential weapons and equipment that the Sri Lankan armed forces needed. The shopping list included air defence weapons, artillery guns, Nishant UAVs (unmanned aerial vehicles) and laser designators for PGMs (precision-guided munitions).

Initially, New Delhi was non-committal.

Top officials involved in the talks on either side told me that in its typical bureaucratic style, New Delhi neither said yes nor said no to the visiting Sri Lankans. So the two brothers went back slightly disappointed but were still hopeful of getting Indian help.

Outwardly, India did adopt a hands off policy vis-à-vis the Sri Lanka conflict. But that was because of domestic political compulsions born out of the fact that the ruling United Progressive Allliance (UPA) government in New Delhi was dependent upon the DMK party from Tamil Nadu for its survival in the Parliament.

Aware of DMK chief M. Karunanidhi's soft corner for Prabhakaran, the UPA did not think it politically prudent to annoy the DMK patriarch by openly supporting the Sri Lankan government against the LTTE.

So, publicly India maintained that it would not give Sri Lanka any offensive weapons.

Yet, in early 2006 India quietly gifted five Mi-17 helicopters to the Sri Lankan Air Force. The only Indian condition was: these helicopters would fly under Sri Lankan Air Force colors. New Delhi clearly did not want to annoy UPA's Tamil Nadu allies like the DMK unnecessarily.

The Mi-17s were in addition to a Sukanya Class offshore patrol vessel (OPV) gifted by the Indian Coast Guard to the Sri Lankan Navy in 2002.

Sri Lankan defence sources later told me that these helicopters played a major role in several daring missions launched by the Sri Lankan Air Force to rescue the Army's Deep Penetration Units and the eight-man teams whenever they were surrounded by LTTE's counter-infiltration units or when injured soldiers had to be airlifted from deep inside LTTE held territory.

As a senior Sri Lankan Army officer confided in me: "Our soldiers operating behind enemy lines functioned with greater degree of confidence and efficiency in Eelam War IV since they knew these helicopters were always on hand to come to their rescue whenever necessary. This was surely one of the key factors in our Special Forces delivering spectacular results."

But hampered by domestic compulsion, New Delhi could not go beyond such meagre and clandestine transfer of military hardware. And publicly all that India was willing to acknowledge was the supply of low-flying detection "Indra" radars to the Sri Lankan Air Force since this equipment was considered a defensive apparatus.

Colombo, on the other hand, was becoming increasingly restless since an all-out war with the LTTE looked inevitable. Domestic political pressure had also stalled the signing of a Defence Cooperation Agreement between India and Sri Lanka. Although both sides had publicly committed themselves to such an accord in 2004 itself, the DCA never materialized.

Insiders in Sri Lanka's defence establishment reveal that India's insistence on securing exclusive rights to the use of Palaly air base in the Jaffna peninsula was the most contentious point between the two delegations. Colombo saw this demand from India as downright insulting and symptomatic of India's hegemonistic mindset. So the DCA never got off the ground. Ironically, three months after the Eelam War IV ended, India decided to fund the repair and restoration of the Palaly air base in north Sri Lanka.

The Rajapaksa regime was nothing if not shrewd. It knew the past history. It was aware of the dynamics that determined India's domestic politics in the context of Tamil Nadu. It was also conscious of India's anxiety in losing strategic space in Sri Lanka.

But above all, the Rajapaksa brothers were pragmatic enough to realize that Sri Lanka needed India's support in the prosecution of the war against the LTTE, total support from China and Pakistan notwithstanding simply because India was Sri Lanka's next door big neighbor. Colombo could ignore India but only upto a point.

So Mahinda Rajapaksa hit upon an idea of setting up an informal exchange mechanism between New Delhi and Colombo. The President nominated both his brothers Basil (an MP and Presidential Adviser) and Gotabaya, the Defence Secretary along with his own secretary, Lalith Weeratunga as members of an informal yet powerful delegation that would update the Indian government on the latest developments as frequently as possible.

India too reciprocated immediately.

India's National Security Adviser MK Narayanan, Foreign Secretary Shiv Shankar Menon and Defence Secretary Vijay Singh formed the Indian trio.

The two teams interacted frequently both on the phone and by visiting each other. The Sri Lankan trio in fact visited New Delhi at least five times between 2007 and 2009. The Indian delegation made three return visits in the same period.

Most of the interactions were low-profile and discreet except the Indian team's June 2008 trip to Colombo which attracted huge attention mainly because of its timing. That time Sri Lanka's military operation was pushing the LTTE out of its north western coastal areas in the Mannar district.

And two months later, Sri Lanka was supposed to host the 15th summit of the South Asian Association for Regional Cooperation (SAARC).

When Narayanan, Menon and Singh arrived in the Sri Lankan capital in a special Indian Air Force plane, almost unannounced, military analysts both in India and Sri Lanka were speculating a massive retaliatory strike by the LTTE.

Indian intelligence agencies apparently had credible information that such a counter attack could be aimed at the 15th SAARC summit that Colombo was hosting on August 2 and 3.

The India officials wanted to ensure foolproof security for the summit. New Delhi in fact persuaded the Sri Lankan's to accept India's help during the summit. After much persuasion and even a veiled threat that India may stay away from the summit if New Delhi's suggestions on a security upgrade in Colombo was not met, Sri Lanka reluctantly allowed Indian Naval ships, anti-aircraft guns and helicopters to be deployed in and around Colombo for the duration of the meet.

I happened to be in Colombo as part of the media delegation that traveled with Prime Minister Manmohan Singh. I had never seen such tight security in Sri Lanka. The Sri Lankan capital was indeed locked down in a tight security grid for the duration of the summit. The Indian Prime Minister and all top Indian officials were transported in Indian Air Force helicopters from the Bandarnaike International Airport to the heart of Colombo. All roads used by the VIPs were shut hours before they traveled on them. In fact, I remember friends in Colombo having left town to avoid being inconvenienced by the stifling security arrangements.

The SAARC summit did pass off peacefully although, as usual, its focus was hijacked by the hyped meeting between the Indian and Pakistani Prime Ministers.

But security at the SAARC summit was not the only point of discussion that India was interested in. The top Indian officials, according to sources in Colombo, also wanted detailed briefing on the on-going operations in the North. This was readily done at the Ministry of Defence by both the Commander of the Army, General Fonseka and Commander of the Navy, Vice Admiral Karannagoda.

The Indian delegation, I was told by an insider, once again raised the issue of increasing Chinese and Pakistani involvement in Sri Lanka's military campaign but was quietly reminded that it was India's refusal to supply lethal weapons that had compelled Colombo to look elsewhere, primarily to China.

But the most important political message was delivered by the Indian delegation to President Rajapaksa. He was told to try and conclude Eelam War IV before the summer of 2009 when India was expected to hold the general elections for Lower House of the Parliament.

The ruling Congress party obviously did not want the shadow of Sri Lanka's ethnic conflict to fall on the politics of Tamil Nadu and needlessly complicate matters during the election campaign. President Rajapaksa did not commit himself on the deadline but promised to expedite the operations. The trio returned to New Delhi perhaps with a mixed feeling of achieved only part of its objective.

Colombo may have been ambivalent about meeting Indian requests to end the operations before the general elections but the Sri Lankan leadership once again gratefully acknowledged the Indian Navy's contribution in locating and destroying at least 10 'floating warehouses,' owned by the LTTE.

These warehouses or ships of varying sizes were used by the LTTE to store arms, ammunition and even armoured personnel carriers. These ships, which had no names or identification numbers used to remain on high seas for months on end. They were brought near Sri Lankan shores whenever LTTE needed the arms. Smaller ships and crafts were used to transport these arms to the Sea Tiger bases on the East and the West Coast.

Indian and Sri Lankan Navy sources revealed that well-coordinated operations by the two navies between 2006 and 2009 actually broke the backbone of the Sea Tigers.

The Indian Navy, the Sri Lankans said, helped in various ways.

For instance, the Indian Navy's Dorniers based at Ramnad in Tamil Nadu flew regular reconnaissance missions over the seas around Sri Lanka. These Dornier aircraft fitted with high-powered radars scoured the area for ships with suspicious movement and cargo. Whenever such a ship was detected, the Indian Navy passed on the information to the Sri Lankans. The real time intelligence helped Sri Lankan Navy to track and then destroy the LTTE arms consignments.

Once the rogue ships were located, Sri Lankan Navy's OPVs would go after these floating warehouses and destroy them. The Sri Lankan Navy destroyed the first warehouse ship on 17 September 2006, about 120 nautical miles east of the Island. Three more such ships were sunk in early 2007.

Moreover, under an agreement between the two countries, the Indian Navy and the Coast Guard frequently sent out ships to patrol the Palk Strait and the Gulf of Mannar. The presence of warships and Indian Coast Guards Offshore Patrol Vessels acted as a firm deterrence against the Sea Tigers. Indian Naval ships traveling between the East and the West Coast and those going on overseas deployment were also told to look out for rogue vessels. Frequent exchange of information between the two navies resulted in a fine-tuned system that enabled quick remedial action.

Sri Lanka's Navy Chief Admiral Wasantha Karannagoda praised the Indian Navy's role. ''Co-operation with India has been extremely successful in countering the LTTE. Every year, the Indian Navy with the Indian Coast Guard and the Sri Lankan Navy holds four bilateral discussions. We are conducting coordinated patrols with the Indian Navy as well," he said in early 2008.

"The Navy has destroyed almost all LTTE vessels that could have assisted the Tigers in attacking the armed forces," he said. ''Within one year we have destroyed eight floating warehouses, which had carried more than 10,000 tons of war-like material including artillery, mortar, dismantled parts of three aircrafts, bullet proof vehicles, underwater delivery vehicles, scuba diving sets, and radar, among other things."

In one instance, accurate intelligence enabled the Sri Lankan Navy to sail nearly 1,600 nautical miles southeast of the country, close to coasts of Australia and Indonesia, to destroy three ships on 10-11 September 2007 and a fourth ship, which had escaped the initial action, three weeks later on 7 October, Admiral Karrannnagoda said.

One of the LTTE weapons smuggling vessels was intercepted and destroyed by Naval Task units after a long hot pursuit in the high seas

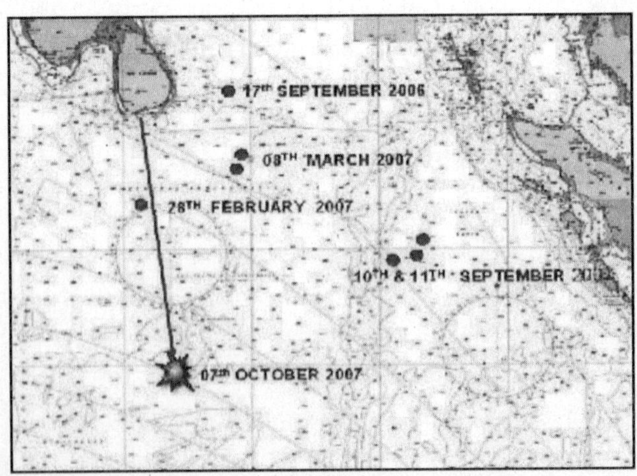

1,700 km off Dondra Head, the southern extremity of Sri Lanka. At least 12 Tamil Tigers on board were killed in the attack.

"We went near to Australian waters and whacked the last four vessels," the Vice- Admiral Karannagoda told *Jane's Navy International* in March 2009. "Yet we are not a big navy; we had to improvise and use innovation and ingenuity to get our job done. The SLN (Sri Lankan Navy) does not possess any frigate-sized ships, so we used offshore patrol vessels and old tankers, merchant vessels and fishing trawlers as support vessels."

What he left unsaid, according to sources in both Indian and Sri Lankan navies, was India's hidden hand in providing vital intelligence and operational support to identify and locate these ships. In March 2009, the Sri Lankan Naval chief deliberately avoided mentioning India's crucial contribution since electioneering in Tamil Nadu was picking up speed and Eelam War IV was in its final stage that month. Any public admission of India's hand in destruction of LTTE assets would have created a furore in Tamil Nadu and futher strained the already delicate relationship between Sri Lanka and India.

But the fact remains that in late 2007 the Indian Navy's Southern Command deployed three fast attack boats and a missile corvette that patrolled the Palk Strait, searched and caught hold of LTTE fugitives. The "sea denial" and "naval blockade" by the Indian Navy started after a daring attack by the Sea Tigers on the Delft Island near Jaffna.

Delft Island, the largest inhabited island of the Jaffna peninsula, is located almost equidistant from Rameswaram in Tamil Nadu and Jaffna. The Sri Lankan Navy used the island to monitor sea and air movements not only towards Jaffna but also between Mannar and Tamil Nadu coast. In May 2007, the Sea Tigers mounted a daring attack on the naval attachement posted at the Delft Island and after killing seven naval personnel took away two anti aircraft machine guns, two machine guns, one RPG launcher and eight rifles.

Some reports said the Sea Tigers also took away functioning radar from the island. Jolted by this setback, the Sri Lankan Navy requested

India for operational help. The assistance was immediately given but both sides had decided to keep quiet about the details.

Despite such a close working relations between the two navies, India was not happy with Colombo's increasing dalliance with China and Pakistan. New Delhi was acutely aware of the deep inroads made by Pakistan and China in India's backyard.

A worried Narayanan had bluntly declared in May 2007: "It is high time that Sri Lanka understood that India is the big power in the region and ought to refrain from going to Pakistan or China for weapons, as we are prepared to accommodate them within the framework of our foreign policy." Which in effect meant India could only supply 'defensive' equipment to Colombo.

Narayanan's statement in fact reflected the dilemma that New Delhi faced. The crisis was of course purely India's own making. Crippled by the iron grip wielded by the DMK and other smaller Tamil parties on the UPA coalition at the Centre, New Delhi could not even openly approve of Colombo's determination to exterminate the LTTE.

Colombo understood India's predicament but had no other option but to shop for weapons and ammunition from elsewhere once India refused to comply with its requests.

Army Commander Sarath Fonseka admitted as much in an interview to me: "It is only after India told us that it cannot supply offensive weapons that we looked at other options. We first tried western countries but their weapons are expensive. Also the Western countries cannot be depended upon to continue the supplies when it came to the crunch as it happened with us in the middle of the war when certain countries blocked supply of spare parts for our airplanes and helicopters. So we turned to China which offered us arms immediately and on favorable terms. They gave us five-year long credit line. We bought armored personnel carriers, artillery pieces, basic infantry weapons and some ammunition from them. As for Pakistan, we only bought some emergency ammunition from them."

Even Defence Secretary Gotabaya Rajapaksa had a similar story to relate.

Little wonder then that Beijing and Islamabad took full advantage of India's quandary.

By February 2007, Gotabaya Rajapaksa had concluded several defence purchase agreements with China.

One of the earliest agreements in Eelam War IV was a $37.6 million deal with China's Poly Technologies in April 2006 to supply its defence forces with ammunition and ordnance for the army and navy. Another company, China National Electronics Import Export Corp supplied a JY 11 3D radar for $5 million.

According to the UK-based *Jane's Defence Weekly* the Sri Lankan navy's requirement, valued at $2.7 million, includes a range of ammunition including 100,000 14.5 mm cartridges, 2,000 RPG-7 rockets and 500 81 mm airburst mortar shells was met by the Chinese. According to the authoritative Defence Weekly, other arms included 50 Type 82 14.5 mm twin-barrel naval guns, 200 Type 85 12.7 mm heavy machine guns, 200 Type 80 7.62 mm multipurpose machine guns, 1,000 Type 56-2 7.62 mm submachine guns and 1,000 Type 56 7.62 mm submachine guns.

China was not alone in supplying arms to Sri Lanka.

A high-level defence delegation from Islamabad visited Sri Lanka in January 2008 to sell weapons to Colombo.

Pakistan Ordnance Factories chief Lt Gen Syed Sabahat Hussein held detailed discussions with Sri Lanka's security officials, including Defence Secretary. The delegation included senior POF officials, Export Director Usman Ali Bhatti and General Manager Abbas Ali.

POF is Pakistan's largest conventional arms and ordnance facility and its 14 factories and four subsidiaries produce several varieties of armaments for export. These include infantry weapons, tank and aircraft ammunition, anti-aircraft and artillery ammunition, rockets, aerial bombs, hand grenades and mortars.

Getting China's and Pakistan's backing was important for the Rajapaksa government but it also needed to get its own act together at home. So the government and especially Defence Secretary Gotabaya Rajapaksa got down to the task of reorienting the Sri Lankan Air Force and the Sri Lankan Navy, always considered the weakest link in the previous military campaigns.

Chapter 10

Pulling their Weight, Finally

For years the Army was the only force that mattered in Sri Lanka. The Sri Lankan Air Force, in the words of an IPKF veteran, was largely a transport wing of the army used to ferry troops and equipment in the late 80's when Indian troops were operating in Sri Lanka. Even after IPKF departed and the Sri Lankan army fought two more Eelam Wars in the 1990s, the Air Force was largely seen as ineffectual.

Veteran journalists and a long time Sri Lanka watcher, PK Balachandran recalls: "In the past, the Air Force was afraid of night flying, was scared of the LTTE's anti-aircraft guns and was not willing to take any chances over the jungles of Wanni. But in Eelam War IV, the Air Force reedemed its reputation by not only providing close air support to the Army's frontline units but also by adopting an aggressive posture on its own in various missions targeted at the LTTE's valuable human and material assets."

The Sri Lankan Navy was in even worse position. Seen largely as a ceremonial force which had consistently come out second best to the innovative, aggressive and ruthless Sea Tigers, the Navy was never really factored in Sri Lanka's battle plans. But all that was before 2003.

By an extraordinary quirk of fate, just before Eelam War IV began, the Air Force and the Navy were headed by two exceptional officers—Air Chief Marshal Roshan Goonatileke and Vice Admiral Wasantha Karannagoda—at the same time. Both are proud of their respective service and both believed that they could make a difference to the war, given the right backing. And that patronage came in the form of Gotabaya Rajapaksa. The Defence Secretary had seen enough action in his earlier career as an army officer to realize that the absence of synergy between the three forces had often cost the Sri Lankan state a decisive military victory in the past.

So, as soon as he took over, Gotabaya Rajapaksa conferred with the Air and Navy chiefs and gave them a carte blanche to revamp and resurrect the two arms. Fortunately for him, both the chiefs responded with new and effective tactics.

The Navy in particular, had to come up with strategies that not only prevented LTTE's replenishment ships from reaching the rebels but also neutralize the attack capability of the Sea Tigers. While po-active and aggressive patrolling backed by 'sea denial' and 'sea blockade' provided by the Indian Navy in the outer periphery of Sri Lanka's maritime domain helped in a big way, the Sri Lankan Navy excelled itself in developing and implementing a completely new method to demolish the Sea Tigers.

After taking over as the Navy Chief in 2005, Adm. Karannagoda analysed the navy's weaknesses. He realized that the heavier Dvora FACs or Fast Attack Crafts were no match for small, fast moving and lightly crewed boats of the Tigers in shallower seas.

The Fast Attack Crafts did form the spearhead of the Sri Lankan Navy but the FACs do not come cheap. Each of them costs anything between $13 million and $15 million. The Navy did not have an unlimited budget and yet it had bought over 30 FACs since 2003. While the powerful FACs were an asset in deep sea, the big boats were helpless against the 'swarming tactics,' used by the Sea Tigers in storming the FACs. Often it was difficulty for the FACs to evade the small suicide boats employed by the Sea Tigers coming straight at them. And losing even one FAC was a double whammy for the Navy. Apart from the expensive loss of FAC, the navy lost over a dozen well-trained and experienced crew members when an FAC was destroyed by the Sea Tigers. For a small Navy these losses were unacceptable.

Admiral Karranaggoda and his senior officers then hit upon the idea of building a fleet of small in-shore Patrol Vessels (IPVs). By mid 2007, after months of carefully balancing the boat, engine, weapons and armor, the "Arrow Boat" was created. The weight and firepower were well balanced resulting in a highly stable, agile boats with maximum firepower.

The new boats were similar to the Sea Tiger boats with a light hull and outboard engines. They could fight close to the shoreline and in shallow waters. Standard infantry weapons such as MPMGs and LMGs are used for enhanced firepower. Two new units were created with these boats: The SBS or Small Boat Squadron and the Rapid Action Boat Squadron or RABS. The Rapid Action Boat Squadron, manned by three men each provided much of the firepower while the Special Boat Squadron engaged in strategic maneuvers against the cluster of LTTE boats.

At sea, the IPCs operated in groups of four crafts. Several groups— totalling 25-30 craft—combined to form IPC squadrons, which were based at strategically important locations around Sri Lanka. The IPC squadrons were organized for rapid-reaction interception operations. While these units got deployed closer to land, the heavier FACs were given special duties in the rough choppier seas. By adopting these measures, the Navy created a double layer around the coastal areas. The outer ring of security was left to the bigger Indian ships that patrolled both the Palk Strait and the Gulf of Mannar.

Talking to *Jane's Navy International*, in March 2009, Admiral Karranggoda said: "Creating the two new units made a huge dent in LTTE operations as they were much better trained than previous crews."

JNI reported that the SBS was trained by the Indian Marine Commandos (MARCOS), US Green Berets and US Navy SEALs. It said RABS personnel were also trained to a high standard and comprised about 400 personnel, mostly those unable to make it through the selection phase for the SBS but still with sufficient levels of physical fitness and the capacity to develop their skills.

According to JNI, all naval officers attend basic training at the Naval and Maritime Academy in Trincomalee, which also provides advanced training for sailors. After basic training, all officers went abroad to Australia, Bangladesh, India, Pakistan, the UK or the US for specialization in communications, gunnery, hydrography and navigation.

The SBS was established in October 2005 with 36 personnel and now numbers 600. It is the SLN's elite force, possessing high levels of physical fitness and advanced training in both land and sea warfare tactics. In a short period of four years, the SBS and RABS proved their usefulness by choking the LTTE's sea-based strength and cutting off whatever arms replenishments the Tigers used to receive from abroad. The Navy for the first time played an equally important part in Sri Lanka's war against the LTTE.

If the Navy redeemed itself admirably in Eelam War IV, the Air Force too played a decisive role in eliminating the LTTE as a military force. The Air Force carried out over 3000 missions in the 33 month war.

The main air strikes were carried out by three jet squadrons that the Sri Lankan Air Force has: The No. 10 squadron comprising Isreali Kfirs planes, the No. 12 operated by the Russian-made MIGs and the No. 5 made up by the Chinese F-7 aircraft. The helicopter fleet consisting of Mi-17s, Mi-24s and Bell choppers also played a crucial part in pinning down the Tigers and preventing any counter-strike by the LTTE.

The Mi 24 gunship squadron based at Hingurakgoda just north of Vavuniya in fact flew over 400 missions in the Northern and Eastern theatres. Known as the No 09 squadron, the helicopters in this fleet carried out several coordinated attacks directed at fortified LTTE positions situated close to the Sri Lankan army's own forward locations.

In an interview with *The Island*, Wing Commander Sampath Thuycontha, Commanding Officer of the squadron said the LTTE hit the choppers several times when the flyers were operating deep inside LTTE-held territory. "Some times, damaged choppers had to come down in areas where fighting was raging," he said but added that the engineering section always responded swiftly and decisively to any emergency. Because of the coordination between the flyers and the maintenance staff, the squadron's operations were never halted despite the LTTE trying its best to cripple the helicopters, the Commanding Officer revealed.

According to *The Island's* knowledgeable Defence Correspondent Shaminda Ferdinando, the Mi-24 squadron, which comprises about 35 officers and 375 men, caused devastation throughout the Wanni theatre.

The Commanding Officer recalled that the Mi-24 squadron played a major role in rescuing at least four LRRP (Long Range Reconnaissance Patrols) teams sent on daring missions into LTTE-held territory. He said that LRRP teams took on high profile targets deep inside enemy held territory both east and west of the A-9 Highway. "Often we flew away under LTTE fire after having landed and taken in the LRRP teams onboard deep inside the war zone," he said.

Squadron Leader Chandana Liyanage, chief engineer of the No 09 squadron recalled how the technicians managed to save a badly hit Mi 24 after it landed in the Iranamadu area in the midst of a ground battle. "Had our technicians failed to fly it again within hours, we would have been forced to destroy it," he said. After preliminary repairs, the damaged chopper was safely flown to the Vavuniya air base.

This dedication and daring shown by the pilots and technicians was in sharp contrast to the Sri Lankan air forces' earlier track record when flyers were seen to be afraid of venturing into the LTTE held areas.

The fighters squadrons played a different role. They usually softened up the targets before a ground offensive. In several cases, the jets pounded known LTTE defence lines, took out some of the artillery guns before the troops moved in. Apart from the killer punch that the Air Force jets often landed on the Tiger bases, the constant missions put the LTTE leadership on tenterhooks and prevented many of its top leaders from moving about freely. Among the best known air attacks was the killing of the LTTE political wing leader SP Tamilselvan in an air raid on his headquarters in Killinochchi.

What is not so well known is that the Sri Lankan Air Force jets almost killed Vellupillai Prabhakaran in one of the air raids on his hideout in Puththukudirippu. But as luck would have it, Prabhakaran had left the base minutes before the bombs rained on the target. Reportedly five MiG 27s, four Kfirs and three F7s were deployed to engage two targets in the Wanni area after reports of his presence had been sent out by intelligence operatives on the ground. Prabhakaran could be at either one of the locations.

The biggest contribution of the Sri Lankan Air Force was however in the use of Isreali-made Unmanned Aerial Vehicles (UAVs). The drones played a major part in keeping a hawk's eye on the battleground and provided enough intelligence on the activity of the LTTE cadres. The UAVs also came in handy when the Sri Lankan government was trying to ascertain the movement of lakhs of Tamil civilians held hostage by the LTTE in the last few months of the war.

Images obtained by the UAVs in mid-April 2009 in fact helped the Sri Lankan government to determine the exact location of civilians and take appropriate action to rescue them.

In the final hours of the battle that killed Prabhakaran and other top LTTE leaders in the vicinity of the Nanthikadal lagoon, Air Chief Marshal Goonetilleke had stationed two MiGs at China Bay air base, very close to the Eastern Coast. The Air Force, wanted to cut down reaction time to a bare minimum in event of a remote possibility of the top LTTE leadership trying to escape the area.

The Sri Lankan Air Force had indeed come a long way from its inglorious days in the 1990s when it lost three aircrafts to the LTTE's ground fire in the assault on Jaffna.

And if the Indians quietly helped the Sri Lankan Navy transform itself, the Sri Lankan Air Force got a big boost from the Chinese and the Pakistanis. Pakistani personnel helped the Sri Lankans in training and maintenance while the Chinese supplied them with vital equipment at a critical time.

In January 2008, the Chinese in fact gifted four F7 GS fighter planes. These aircraft are the most sophisticated jets in Sri Lanka's arsenal today with in-built air interception radar and carry four heat seeking missiles. In fact, it was an F7 plane that shot down one of LTTE's light aircraft over Iranapalai in 2008.

As the operations in the North gathered momentum, both the Air Force and the Navy were increasingly called in to bolster the Army's march towards Killinochchci and Mullaitivu, the LTTE's remaining strongholds.

CHAPTER 11

The March to Mullaitivvu

Once Pooneryn fell in mid-November 2008, Army Commander Gen. Sarath Fonseka decided to launch a three-pronged assault on Killinochchi, the de facto administrative capital of the Tigers.

Strategically located on the A-9 Highway, close to the Elephant Pass, Killinochchi had emerged as the nerve centre for the LTTE government that ruled Wanni with an iron hand post-2000.

Although Prabhakaran rarely stayed in Killinochchi most other senior leaders visited the town when required. The political wing of the outfit first led by SP Tamilselvan and later by B. Nadesan however operated out of here. Before he was killed in a Sri Lankan Air Force raid, Tamilselvan used to receive international mediators, representatives of International NGOs and media persons in Killinochchi. The LTTEs Peace Secretariat, basically a liaison office, also used to function in the town.

Fonseka decided to deploy four divisions—53, 55, 57 and 58—for the multi-pronged attack on Killinochchi.

The 57 Division was tasked to attack the LTTE defence line from Iranamadu Tank to Akkarayankulam via Adampan east of the A-9 Highway and the 58 Division, which had been marched a long way from Mannar to recapture the A-32 Highway on the West Coast was assigned the stretch from Adampan to Jaffna lagoon.

The 55 Division, based north of the Elephant Pass in the Jaffna Peninsula began its advance from north, while the 53 Division launched the troops from the South of the A-9 Highway.

A week after the assault began all four divisions ran into the fiercest resistance during Eeelam War IV. The LTTE summoned its most battle-hardened units to defend Killinochchi and asked its top commanders like Theepan, Bhanu, and Jerry to take charge on various fronts. On one particular day in December, advancing Sri Lankan troops reported half a dozen waves of LTTE assaults in less than 24 hours. In what seemed a hark back to the tactics of the yore, the Tigers rained non-stop heavy artillery and mortar fire on the advancing Army soldiers in an effort to halt the march and may be spread panic in the ranks. But this Sri Lankan army was different and the leadership, unlike the earlier commanders, was prepared to take losses as long the final objective was achievable.

The 3 Brigades of the 58 Division were given the task of assaulting the six mile stretch of heavy Tiger defences from Jaffna lagoon to Adampan, across the Pooneryn-Paranthan road.

But the task was not easy. Heavy north-east monsoon rains had made the terrain unsuitable for the armored regiment's movement. The Pooneryn-Paranthan B-69 Road cut through two different types of terrain. On its north, the land is mainly marshy while vast, open paddy fields dot the areas south of the B-69 Highway. Overflowing streams and rivers slowed down the troops. Often soldiers waded through chest deep water or were forced to negotiate knee-deep slush even as they faced continuous LTTE fire.

To add to their problems, soldiers also came under attack by Sea Tiger units who tried to join the battle by infiltrating from the Jaffna Lagoon. That's when the Mi-24 helicopter gunships got into the action to beat back the Sea Tigers.

On the other hand, the 55 and 53 Divisions based at Muhamalai, Nagar Kovil and Kilali north of the Elephant Pass had to fight extremely hard to capture the strategically important Muhamalai Forward Defence Line (FDL) of the LTTE.

This was made possible by the successful behind the line infiltration carried out by several eight-man teams and Deep Penetration Units. Brigadier Prasanna Silva, GOC of the 55 Division and 53 Division Commander Brigadier Kamal Gunaratne knew that the LTTE would put up its stiffest resistance at the strategic Elephant Pass and had therefore decided to employ the elements of the elite Air

Mobile Brigade and the Mechanized Infantry Brigade to support the Infantry's advance.

The intensity of the fight north of the Elephant Pass can be gauged by the fact that it took the 53 and 55 Divisions nearly a week to advance just 800 metres and capture the LTTE's first defence line. Of course, like the 58 Division, troops of these two Divisions were also bogged down by heavy rains lashing the areas that December. And the LTTE was not willing to give up so easily. Both sides suffered heavy fatalities in these battles but the LTTE, unlike the Army, was now falling short of able-bodied young men and women to replenish its depleting ranks.

The 57 Division however had the most difficult task of assaulting the main defence line protecting Killinochchi along its southern side. The 57 Division troops launched two separate operations at the same earth bund north of Puthumurippu Kulam and Therumurikandi. They captured about 1.2 km stretch on the earth bund that runs across the A-9 road.

To put additional pressure on LTTE's defences, Fonseka ordered the 59 Division operating North of Weli Oya to advance further northwards and push back the LTTE defence line. The 59 Division maneuvers meant Prabhakaran could not release his fighters defending Mullaitivvu to go and reinforce the Killinochchi front which had come under tremendous pressure by the middle of December 2008.

By December 20, the Fonseka had stretched the LTTE resources so much that senior Tiger commanders were forced to shuttle between different fronts to motivate and give direction to the new recruits who were being killed by the dozens. Radio intercepts heard by the Army's Signal Intelligence units suggested that the Tigers were forced to replace the area commander named Lawrence, in-charge of defences south of Killinochchi by Swarnam, earlier heading the special forces unit of the LTTE. However Swarnam himself had failed to defend Batticaloa in the Eastern Province in 2007 in the face of the Army's onslaught there.

Task Force III, which was operating in support of the 57 Division was now after Swarnam and other senior commanders, harassing them by surprise and swift raids deep into the LTTE held territory. In mid-December, one of the units under Task Force III almost captured Swarnam alive during an offensive north of Mankulam area.

One day troops operating behind the enemy lines suddenly noticed that two green colored trucks had arrived in their vicinity. Three motorcycles were escorting the truck. Troops realized that some one important was touring the area and sure enough, the platoon commander suddenly saw Swarnam stepping out of the vehicle.

The soldiers, sensing a golden opportunity to kill a very senior LTTE leader, opened fire but the alert Tigers immediately fired back and whisked away Swarnam in another vehicle. It was a narrow escape for the senior LTTE commander.

By now, a new element was being added to the fighting. Civilians, living in the vicinity of Paranthan and clusters close to east and south of Killinochchi were proving to be a major hurdle for the soldiers. LTTE had started using these civilian inhabitations to hide artillery guns and mortars and fire at the advancing troops. Large civilian presence was preventing the soldiers from firing back but in certain cases, when the Tiger cadres suddenly popped up from behind a house and attacked soldiers, troops fired back in an almost reflexive action. The hapless civilians were now getting caught in the crossfire.

The new impediment had now popped up for the commanders. Civilians were being used as human shield by retreating LTTE fighters. The Army was aware that the Tigers had forced much of the population in earlier living in Mannar Rice Bowl and along the Pooneryn-Paranthan road, to fall back with them as they retreated from the north-western areas towards Killinochchi. But there was no clarity on how many people were being shifted by the LTTE. Through much of November and December, the numbers that were being cited were in the region of 80,000 to 100,000 people-young, old, sick, men, women, children—who were forced to leave their homes with bare minimum belongings.

As the Army advanced deeper into LTTE territory, it was becoming apparent that troops would increasingly face the choice between killing LTTE combatants and sparing the civilians. Some times however civilians made the Army's task easier by simply risking their lives and escaping the LTTE's clutches. On Christmas Day for instance, the defence ministry website *defence.lk* reported that a group of civilians had run away from the LTTE and sought shelter with the Army.

Twenty-one Tamil civilians including 9 children who were able to escape the LTTE's grip reached security forces controlled area in Kokkuthuduwai, Mullaittivu. The group of Tamil escapees, 8 elderly males and 4 elderly females of 4 families, reached security forces around 7.15 a.m., the ministry said.

Defence.lk quoted the elderly people as saying: "LTTE has accelerated child recruitment as they are running short of manpower; we want to save our children from the LTTE."

Another bigger group of over 200 people stumbled out into government controlled area south of Mankulama, seeking protection with the Army. These intermittent civilian arrivals forced the government to set up relief camps at various points. Little did the army know that this trickle would turn into a deluge in less than four months.

In Colombo, President Mahinda Rajapaksa and Defence Secretary Gotabaya were coming under pressure from humanitarian agencies, countries like India and the United States to ensure that civilians were not hurt. The government told the worried international community that it was the LTTE that was actually holding people hostage. President Rajapaksa however told the Army to ensure maximum safety for the non-combatants.

The UN was also concerned.

In an appeal issued in the fourth week of December John Holmes, the UN's Under-Secetary-General for Humanitarian Affairs and UN Emergency Relief Coordinator called on the LTTE to allow civilians to be able to move freely to areas where they felt most secure. He also asked the Government to receive newly displaced people according to internationally agreed principles.

"As fighting surrounds the areas towards which families have been displaced, and with few choices about where to move, they are increasingly susceptible to harm due to the fighting," John Holmes said in the statement."

"While they have had access to basic food, in large part due to the Government and the UN assistance transported through the lines of fighting," he said, "they have few, if any, reserves and the conditions of their basic shelter, water and sanitation are increasingly inadequate as many have been displaced multiple times over the last months, weeks and days."

At that point the UN Office for the Coordination of Humanitarian Affairs estimated that around 230,000 people had been displaced due to intensified fighting in the north of the country during the second half of 2008.

Even as this crisis rose, the rains eased a little in the third week of December and the battles resumed in right earnest across multiple fronts.

On December 24, Task Force III troops advancing north of Ampakamam near the Iranamadu tank discovered an airstrip built by the LTTE after clearing a thick forest.

The airstrip had a 25m wide and 350 m long runway. This was the third airstrip captured by the Sri Lankan troops. The first one was overrun by troops of 57 Division in Panikkankulam area while the second was captured by the 58 Division in the Nivil area. But there was still no sign of any aircraft that the Tigers were supposed to possess.

On Christmas Day, Army chief Gen. Sarath Fonseka flew to Vavuniya to review the battle plans. Major General Jagath Jayasuriya, Commander, Security Forces Headquarters Wanni briefed him about the situation. In attendance were all the divisional and brigade commanders. The meeting was significant since the Army looked poised to enter Killinochchi although the LTTE resistance was at its fiercest in this phase of the war.

A day after the high-level conference, Air Force jets started strafing LTTE positions along the bunds and specifically targeted heavy vehicles engaged in earth-bund construction in the Iranamadu and Paranthan areas.

As the world prepared to bid goodbye to 2008, troops of the 58 Division led by Brig (now Maj. Gen) Shavindra Silva entered

Paranthan junction, after overcoming the last of LTTE defences in the area. Over 30 LTTE cadres were killed in the final confrontation on December, 31.

Paranthan, about 4.5 km from Killinochchi, is one of the most crucial intersections on the arterial A-9 Highway that connects south and north Sri Lanka. The junction connects four important locations, Killinochchi to the south, Pooneryn to the west, Mullaitivvu to the east and the Elephant Pass, considered the gateway to Jaffna, in the north.

With Paranthan under its control, the Army could now march towards Elephant Pass, 9 km to the north and launch a pincer movement against the LTTE's Elephant Pass Garrison. Similarly, the Army could now encircle Killinochchi from three directions.

Even as the Army laid a siege to Killinochchi, LTTE's political head B. Nadesan told an international news agency that the outfit had made a strategic withdrawal from Paranthan.

"We have made several strategic withdrawals in order to save the lives of our people and maintain the strength of our forces. When the time and place is conducive, we will regain the land we have lost," he told Associated Press.

In the email interview, Nadesan again said that LTTE was ready for peace talks with Government. But the government was hardly interested.

Just a week before Nadesan's interview, President Rajapaksa had ruled out any possibility of a ceasefire or negotiations with the LTTE.

If capturing Paranthan was a major victory for the Sri Lankan army, a bigger and symbolically important triumph was to come just 48 hours later.

On 2nd January 2009, the 57 and 58 Division troops entered Killinochchi town, LTTEs administrative hub for over a decade.

The 57 Division troops lead by Major General Jagath Dias entered Killinochchi from the South and Southwestern boundaries while Brigadier Shavindra Silva's 58 Division marched in from the North and Northwest.

Although Killinochchi was not very important in military-strategic terms, its capture had a great symbolic value for the Sri Lankan state. Killinochchi had changed hands twice in the past 20 years. In 1990, the Sri Lankan army had withdrawn its garrison allowing the LTTE to take over the town. In 1996 the Army again regained control of Killinochchi during operations Sathjaya I, II, and III but in 1998 the LTTE was back in-charge of the town. Since then Killinochchi had been designated the de facto capital of Eelam.

The recapture of Killinochchi was a matter of joy for President Rajapaksa. He had embarked on a big gamble to take the LTTE head on and led the country into, what, to many seemed an impossible war to win. But the security forces didn't let him down. Little wonder that he announced the conquest of Killinochchi personally.

"A short while ago, our brave and heroic troops have fully captured Killinohchi that was considered the main bastion of the LTTE. Our troops have completely taken over the fortress of the LTTE that has been described by our own leaders and accepted internationally as the most powerful terrorist organization in the world."

"Whatever the words or language used to describe it, this is truly an incomparable victory. What our heroic troops have achieved is not only the capture of the great fortress of the LTTE, but a major victory in the world's battle against terrorism. The entire world must today appreciate the outstanding success of the Sri Lankan troops," President Rajapaksa told the entire top brass of the government at a specially convened meeting in Colombo's Presidential secretariat.

The LTTE had a vice-like grip over Wanni and particular Killinochchi but all the government functionaries–postmasters, government agent, doctors, teachers–were on the pay roll of the Sri Lankan government. But willy-nilly, they were all under the LTTE's thumb.

And yet, when Army troops entered Killinochchi not a single soul was in sight.

True to Nadesan's words, the LTTE had totally emptied the town. In what is termed a strategic withdrawal but in reality was a desperate measure, the LTTE had retreated into the jungles of Mullaitivvu along with the entire civil population and government bureaucracy!

I remember landing in Killinochchi a fortnight after it was recaptured. The first thing that struck me was how empty and devastated the town looked. Not a single civilian in sight; buildings pock-marked with bullet holes; offices and houses without roofs. Killinochchi hardly looked like the de facto capital of the LTTE that it was for over a decade.

The LTTE's erstwhile peace secretariat and Tamilselvan's office were now converted into barracks for soldiers. We were taken on a tour of the area and shown the underground bunkers that were built inside the LTTE headquarters, the highly sophisticated communication equipment left behind by the retreating LTTE cadres and the place where Tamilselvan was killed in the Sri Lankan Air Force bombing raid.

We also traveled to Paranthan and then to the iconic Elephant Pass. The serenity at the pass which is nothing but a narrow isthmus connecting the mainland with the Jaffna Peninsula, was deceptive. Just a week ago, it had been the scene of one of Eelam War IV's fiercest battles. Now as the Sri Lankan flag fluttered in the high wind, a lonely armored personnel carrier stood near the dilapidated board that had the barely visible words 'Elephant Pass' inscribed in stone.

After the fall of Killinochchi, Prabhakaran and his top commanders had perhaps reckoned that the Sri Lankan army would hesitate to enter the forests since the jungles of Mullaitivvu had proved to be a quagmire for the defence forces in the past. Moreover, Prabhakaran was likely to have counted on the Western governments and human rights organizations to raise the issue of civilian populations safety in the battle ahead. Colombo was aware of such a possibility and had accordingly devised counter-measures by deploying some of the smartest diplomats to convey Sri Lanka's fight against the LTTE.

Even as the government braced for further pressure from the international community, the Army was relentlessly marching forward overrunning LTTE defences and heavily-fortified positions. In less than a week after entering Killinochchi, the final two-pronged attack on the Elephant Pass Garrison was mounted. By January 9, troops of the 53 Division commanded by Brigadier Kamal Gunarathne and 55 Division Commanded by Brigadier Prasanna Silva advancing from Jaffna-Muhamali and Kilali north of the Elephant Pass linked up with the rampaging soldiers of the 58 Division pressing forward from to south to north. In the process the three divisions simply smashed the hitherto impregnable LTTE defences around the Elephant Pass.

The capture of Elephant Pass after nearly a decade brought the entire Kandy-Jaffna A-9 Road under the Sri Lankan Government's control.

But the victorious march was tempered with the realization that the real battle now lay ahead since civilians were increasingly getting sucked in the cross-fire. A day after the conquest of the Elephant Pass, in fact came the news that seven innocent Tamils trying to escape the LTTE area were killed in the firing by the Tigers when they attempted to cross over into government-controlled area. The incident occurred east of Murrusomodai and Kanchipuram. However 50 others including two men injured in the same firing managed to arrive in the Army controlled areas of Paranthan.

The rising civilian death toll had an immediate echo in Tamil Nadu.

Political parties including the ruling DMK started asking for a more forceful intervention by New Delhi. Under pressure, the UPA rushed Foreign Secretary Shiv Shankar Menon to Colombo.

His visit however had very little effect on the conduct of the operations. Menon, a highly respected former Indian High Commissioner to Sri Lanka, forcefully conveyed India's concerns over the safety of the civilians in the battle zone.

The Rajapaksas listened to him patiently and sympathized with the Indian government's predicament but made it clear to the seasoned diplomat that Colombo was in no mood to halt the military campaign, especially at a time when the LTTE was cornered so effectively. A dejected Menon returned to New Delhi almost empty handed.

Over the next fortnight, Sri Lankan Army troops bulldozed their way through several LTTE bases and strongholds like Dharmapuram to finally reach Mullaitivvu on January 25. The 59 Division commanded by Brigadier Nandana Udawatte had come a long way after launching operations from Weli Oya in January 2008. Raised specifically to liberate Mullaitivvu, the 59 Division had fought its way across Anandakulam and Nagacholau forest reserves to reach the outskirts of Mullaitivu in December 2008 but took another month to capture the last LTTE stronghold on the East Coast.

Situated on a narrow stretch of land between the Nanthikandal lagoon and the sea, Mullaittivvu was the LTTE's strongest base in the area. Being close to the coast, Mullaitivvu had emerged as the key coordination centre between the Sea Tigers and the ground based LTTE units. Most of LTTE's supplies, both military hardware and daily essentials for the cadres, were brought in by sea through Mullaitivvu. The Tigers had taken control of the base in 1996 after it had overrun the Army garrison there and killed over 1200 soldiers.

Up North, the 55 Division under Brigadier Prasanna Silva was rapidly moving southwards along the coast closing all escape options for the LTTE leadership. The division had captured the last Sea Tiger base at Chalai, home to LTTE's strongest and most fearsome fighting wing, the Sea Tigers. The Sea Tigers had launched several devastating attacks on the Sri Lankan Navy from the Chalai base in the past. After four days of close combat, several top Sea Tigers leaders were killed. Brigadier Prasanna Silva, a former Special Forces Brigade Commander who had earlier played a major role in the capture of Vakarai in the Eastern province stronghold of the guerrillas, had once again scored a major victory in taking over a strategic Tiger base.

Once the 55 Division linked up with the 59 Division in Mullaitivvu, all escape routes by sea were closed for the LTTE leadership which was now trapped north and south of the Paranthan-Mullaitivu (A-35) road.

The Tigers, in fact, did try to escape by sea on January 20 but an alert Navy foiled the attempt. At least four LTTE boats were sunk off the cost of Mullaitivvu in a fierce gun battle that night. One of the Navy's fast attack craft was damaged in the clash.

Several hundred civilians were meanwhile trickling out of the LTTE controlled areas into government held territory, bringing with them tales of deprivation, hunger and about children and women being forcibly drafted by the Tigers to fight the army. The civilians plight once again raised alarm in New Delhi and this time, External Affairs Minister Pranab Mukherjee personally flew to Colombo to seek protection for civilians from the ongoing conflict.

At India's insistence on January 30, President Rajapaksa issued a 48-hour ultimatum to the LTTE to surrender and allow free movement of civilians trapped in conflict areas so as to allow them to come into government-designated safe zone.

"I urge the LTTE, within the next 48 hours to allow free movement of civilians to ensure their safety and security. For all those civilians, I assure a safe passage to a secure environment. I also assure all those living in the North and in conflict areas in particular," President Mahinda Rajapaksa said in a statement.

At the beginning of February 2009 the Red Cross estimated that over 250,000 civilians were still trapped in the territory still under LTTE control.

The 48-hour deadline came and went but the Tigers refused to relent. The government was now facing a major dilemma. It knew that the LTTE was cornered and trapped in the narrow territory between the East Coast and the Mullaitivvu jungles but it could not launch an all-out attack fearing massive civilian casualties.

The impasse was to last over the next hundred days.

Chapter 12

Making Haste, Slowly

February and March 2009 were perhaps the most frustrating months for the President and the three armed forces. They had reduced the LTTE to an area less than 300 sq km.

This progress was astounding.

In February 2007, Prabhakaran was lord and master of nearly 15,000 sq km of Sri Lanka's territory. The forces had managed to kill over 15,000 Tigers, although they themselves had lost nearly 4,000 soldiers in 30 months of war. And yet, because of the presence of hundreds and thousands of civilians, the Sri Lankans were unable to launch that final decisive push against the Tamil Tigers.

As thousands of trapped Tamil civilians continued to flee the war zone, Sri Lankan troops mounted heavy pressure to overrun Tigers' positions in a major ground offensive. Over 100 LTTE cadres were killed in a close combat fight near an LTTE stronghold located north of A-35 road (Paranthan- Mullaittivu) in the Kuppilankulam area in the first fortnight of February.

Sri Lankan Air Force fighter jets attacked LTTE suicide boats on the beach north of Mullaittivvu, destroying at least half a dozen boats and killing several Sea Tigers.

By mid-February over 35,000 out of an estimated 250,000 Tamil civilians had moved into the government controlled areas.

There were increasing reports that frustrated LTTE cadres were preventing civilians from leaving the Tiger-held areas by firing at them.

In one instance, LTTE cadres fired at civilians attempting to cross over to government territory, killing 19 and injuring 75 in Udayarkattukulam area of Mullaittivvu. Among the dead were two children and five women. In another incident the Tigers fired at a bus transporting civilians out of the war zone killing a woman and injuring 13 others.

They attacked the bus at Puliyankulam while it was traveling to the government-controlled town of Vavuniya. The injured included four elderly women, two boys and two girls.

The biggest incident occurred on February 10 when an LTTE female suicide bomber blew herself up in a refugee centre in Mullaitivvu, killing 29 people, including 10 civilians and injuring 64 others, 40 of them civilians.

Despite these setbacks, troops continued to press ahead and by early March had boxed the LTTE into an area of about 60 sq km. Nearly 50,000 troops of 53, 55, 58 and 59 Divisions had encircled the LTTE positions. Task Force VIII was assisting these divisions.

In the first week of March troops of the 53 and 58 Division and Task Force VIII captured the strategic Puthukkudiyiruppu junction. The town centre was captured after three days of heavy gun-fire and pitched battles as the LTTE had put up heavy defences around the town. LTTE cadres hid in buildings in the middle of the town and kept firing at the troops.

In the end, armored units of the 5th Mechanized Infantry Division were called into destroy the buildings from where troops were taking fire. The armored vehicles that were brought in included T-55 and AM2 Battle Tanks. Having taken control of Puthukkudiyiruppu, the Army's next target was Iranapalai two kilometers north-east of Puthukkudiyiruppu. Military intelligence had credible reports that Prabhakaran along with his senior colleagues Pottu Amman, Bhanu, Theepan, Swarnam and Sea Tiger leader Soosai were holed out at Iranapalai.

The troops were now pushing the remaining Tigers towards northeast of the Mullaitivvu lagoon closer to the government declared

Safe Zone along the sea coast. The 55 division had expanded its operations to the South of Chalai and was positioned 4km to the North of the Puthumathalan safe zone.

But the Tigers were not giving up yet. As battles were raging, a group of at least 20 Sea Tiger boats directed a continuous hail of bullets at the troops from 12.7mm cannons mounted on the boats. Army intelligence reports said that Sea Tiger leader Soosai and leader of the LTTE women's wing, Vidusha were personally directing the attack.

However, the much expected massive counter-attack from the LTTE that would have halted the Army's blitzkrieg was not forthcoming mainly because the Sri Lankan Army moved much more swiftly than the Tigers ever expected. Unlike in the past, when troops used to pause after a major military victory, Gen. Fonseka and his top commanders did not offer any respite to the beleaguered Tigers. The troops just kept going despite having traveled long distances and taken heavy fatalities.

This new approach robbed the Tigers of any respite. The frustration was certainly building up. It showed up in a rare statement from LTTE in early March. The Tigers were reacting to a grand welcome given by the Indian state to Sri Lankan Army Chief Gen. Sarath Foneska during his four-day visit to India in March. Gen. Fonseka met India's top-most military hierarchy, toured important military establishments and briefed Indian leaders on the progress of the operations.

The VIP treatment accorded to Gen. Fonseka rattled the LTTE no end. The statement said: "Is the Indian State attempting yet another historic blunder? The State welcome given by the Indian State to the Sri Lanka military chief Lt. Gen. Sarath Fonseka, who is heading the Sri Lankan State's war of ethnic genocide against the Eelam Tamils, has deeply hurt them. Liberation Tigers of Tamil Eelam (LTTE) strongly condemns the Indian State action of extending a State welcome to the military chief of the Sinhala State which has unilaterally abrogated the ceasefire agreement and has launched widespread military offensives in the Tamil homeland. The Sri Lankan State is facing many warnings and condemnations for its attempt to seek a military solution and for its enormous human rights violations. Despite this, the Sinhala State ignores these warnings and condemnations and continues with its abductions, killings, and arrests of Tamils. The Sinhala State, keen to cover up this truth, is blaming the freedom movement of the Tamils, the LTTE, for the continuation of the war and is seeking assistance from the world for its war of ethnic genocide. Many of the European countries, understanding this hidden motive of the Sinhala State, have halted all assistance that could support the ethnic genocide of the Tamils. The Indian State also knows this truth. Yet, while pronouncing that a solution to the Tamil problem must be found through peaceful means, it is giving encouragement to the military approach of the Sinhala State. This can only lead to the intensification of the genocide of the Tamils. LTTE wishes to point out to the Indian State that by this historic blunder it will continue to subject the Eelam Tamils to misery and put them in the dangerous situation of having to face ethnic genocide on a massive scale. On behalf of the Eelam Tamils, LTTE kindly requests the Tamils of Tamil Nadu to understand this anti-Tamil move of the Indian State and express their condemnation. We did not leave the ceasefire agreement and we did not start the war. We are only undertaking a defensive war against the war of ethnic genocide of the Sri Lankan State.

We still have not abandoned the Norway sponsored peace efforts and we are ready to take part in such efforts. In this context, the Indian States move of propping up the politically-militarily-economically weakened Sri Lankan State has upset Eelam Tamils.

The view expressed by the Indian military chiefs, 'India wants to ensure that the Sri Lankan Army maintains its upper hand over the LTTE', just illustrates the efforts of the Indian State to prop up the Sinhala war machine.

The Indian State must take the responsibility for the ethnic genocide of the Tamils that will be carried out by the Sinhala military re-invigorated by such moves of the Indian State."

As if on cue, pro-LTTE political parties in Tamil Nadu started protesting against India's Sri Lanka policy. In a joint statement issued on March 13 following a three-hour consultations on the Sri Lankan issue at a hotel in Chennai, PMK founder S Ramadoss and VCK President Thol Thirumavalavan accused the Central Government of sabotaging Tamil aspirations on the Sri Lankan issue by lending support to the military-backed genocide of the Eelam Tamils. Ramadoss and Thirumavalavan demanded "an immediate halt to all Indian military aid to the Sinhalese chauvinist regime in Sri Lanka which has directed its entire strength in a barbaric manner against the Tamil people."

But neither New Delhi nor Colombo was unduly bothered.

Over the next fortnight the Army intensified its operations and in the first week of April killed over 500 Tigers including several senior leaders like Theepan, Ruben, Nagesh, Gadaphi, Prabhakaran's former bodyguard and two seniormost female Tigers, Vidusha and Kamalini.

"The only uncleared area left for the remaining LTTE cadres and leaders are the no-fire zone," military spokesman Brigadier Udaya Nanayakkara said that time. This was the first time that troops were able to kill such a large number of LTTE leaders in one battle, the Brigadier recalled.

Significantly, troops in Puthukkudiyiruppu found personal documents of LTTE Leader Prabhakaran from a well fortified bunker in the area. Prabhakarans birth certificate and his family album were among the documents recovered by the troops from an underground bunker, believed to be the LTTE's operations room before the leaders fled the area.

By the end of April first week, the 20 sq km No Fire Zone came under intense media and international scrutiny. The condition of the civilians remained a matter of big concern for both Colombo and the international community.

On April 11, the Tokyo Co-Chairs (U.S., European Union, Norway and Japan) called upon the LTTE to release civilians trapped in the No-Fire Zone. In a statement, the US Embassy in Colombo said:

"Co-Chair members expressed urgent concern for the safety of more than a hundred thousand people trapped by the conflict between government forces and the Liberation Tigers of Tamil Eelam (LTTE) in a narrow strip of land in northern Sri Lanka. They call on the Tamil Tigers to permit freedom of movement for the civilians in the area. They discussed the need for the Sri Lankan government and the LTTE to respect the No Fire Zone and protect the civilians trapped there. They reaffirmed the need to stop shelling into the No Fire Zone to prevent further civilian casualties. They stressed the importance of a humanitarian pause and of ensuring that adequate supplies of food, water and medicine reach the civilians in the zone. Assistant Secretary Boucher and the other Co-Chair representatives discussed how to best end the futile fighting without further bloodshed."

India too pressured President Rajapaksa to prevent civilian casualties. Although Colombo had withstood constant pressure for calling a ceasefire with the LTTE, the President, citing the upcoming Sinhala and Tamil New Year days, ordered the Army to pause its offensive operations for 48 hours. The President's Secretariat said in a statement on April 12:

"As the nation celebrates the traditional Sinhala and Tamil New Year, His Excellency the President is deeply conscious of the need to give the civilian population entrapped as hostages by the ruthless actions of the LTTE, the opportunity to celebrate these festivities in a suitable atmosphere and to have uninhibited freedom of movement from the No Fire Zone to the cleared areas.

"With this objective in view, His Excellency has directed the Armed Forces of the State to restrict their operations during the New Year to those of a defensive nature. The Sinhala and Tamil New Year is symbolic of the amity prevailing amongst all communities in Sri Lanka. In the true spirit of the season, it is timely for the LTTE to acknowledge its military defeat and lay down its weapons and surrender. The LTTE must also renounce terrorism and violence permanently."

The LTTE was however in mood to surrender. Prabhakaran was obviously counting on the presence of the large number of civilians to prevent further inroads by the Army but he had reckoned without the people's fears and frustration and the Army's maneuvers as a momentous development just a week down the line showed.

After two days of the futile pause, during which the LTTE neither surrendered nor allowed civilians to cross over into government-held areas, troops resumed their operations but they had to be careful to avoid civilian casualties.

For the ground commanders it was becoming difficult to assess the presence of civilians. That's when the Israeli-made Unmanned Aerial Vehicles (UAVs) operated by the Air Force came to the rescue.

Accurately spotting the gathering of a large number of civilians near a fortification, the Air Force gave the exactly coordinates to the troops of 58 Division. Brig. Shavindra Silvas troops then attacked the LTTE earth bund, neutralized the defences at Puttumathalan just short of the No Fire Zone to create an opening for the trapped civilians to come out.

And come out they did in such overwhelming numbers that the Army immediately called the operation, "the world's largest humanitarian rescue mission in history."

As state television beamed the pictures from the battle front, the world watched in horror and relief. Some 80,000 people, some of them wading through neck-high lagoon water, carrying bundles of belongings, streamed out into the government-controlled area; some were sick and wounded; others were helping or carrying pregnant women. Most were dazed.

President Rajapaksa went on national television and once again told the LTTE to lay down arms or face total annihilation.

On April 21, I flew into Colombo once again and then went to Puttamathalan in an army helicopter two days later. The No Fire Zone was two kilometers away. As we went around the desolate area, thousands of civilians were still in a state of shock.

I met a man who had lost two children aged 5 and 8 during the run for safety. A pregnant mother was not able to locate her husband. An old man named Rajan summed up the previous week:

"We could not move from there. The Tigers were searching everywhere. If they found someone planning to escape they were ordered to immediately shoot them down."

The huge influx created a new problem for the government. Now the number of civilians who had to be housed in relief camps had reached over 180,000.

It was no easy task to provide relief to the Tamils displaced time and again from their homes. For the time being they were sent to a huge relief camp set up by the government at a place called Mainik Farm near the town of Vavuniya.

In time, the number of people there would reach over 200,000.

I visited the camp in the third week of April and found the government was struggling to provide basic amenities like food, shelter and medicine. Sri Lanka's foreign secretary Palitha Kohona, a key diplomat who traveled the world to lobby in Sri Lanka's favor over the previous six months after the war intensified, admitted that the government was facing a massive challenge. "We know that our bigger challenge is to resettle these people but we have done this before in the east and we will do it again," he told me in Colombo.

The Vavuniya camp was just a small part of a big effort planned by the government to rehabilitate the displaced Tamils in the north.

Although everyone knew this could not be a permanent solution, it was certainly a good beginning.

But the world was still not convinced that Sri Lanka was handling the unfolding humanitarian crisis the right way.

Just when the army was ready for the kill, the western world and even India once again put pressure on Sri Lanka to ease the operations.

India in fact sent National Security Adviser MK Narayanan and foreign secretary Shiv Shankar Menon to Colombo again, seeking some kind of pause in operations.

The UPA government had come under more strain as campaigning for the Lok Sabha elections picked up speed and political parties in Tamil Nadu upped the ante seeking effective intervention in Sri Lanka.

It was a tough balancing act for New Delhi.

It did not want the Army operations to stop but it could not ignore the political compulsions either.

Foreign Minister Pranab Mukherjee insisted that India was only concerned about Tamil civilians and not about the LTTE. But local political compulsions often blurred the lines between concern for Tamil civilians and the Tamil Tigers. Even a man as media savvy and politically prudent as Home Minister P. Chidambaram could not help playing to the gallery when he displayed sympathies for the LTTE.

He said in an interview: "We don't wish Prabhakaran ill," at a time when India officially regarded Prabhakaran as a terrorist.

Tamil Nadu Chief Minister M. Karunanidhi went a step further and sat on a farcical fast in Chennai lasting less than four hours forcing Colombo to announce it will not use heavy weapons in the war.

Britain and France also rushed their foreign ministers to try and stop the war but Colombo remained firm.

President Rajapaksa ordered the forces to stop using heavy weapons like the artillery guns and put a halt to aerial bombings but refused to call off the ground operations.

It was already the first week of May 2009 and the endgame in Sri Lanka was in its very last stage.

Troops were now looking for Prabhakaran and his top colleagues. The quest ended in a non-descript mangrove on the banks of Nanthikadal lagoon on May 19. The positive identification of Prabhkaran's body by his former military commander Col. Karuna, officially ended Eelam War IV but Sri Lanka's battle to win the trust and confidence of the Tamils had just begun.

Chapter 13

What Next

On 19th May, Sri Lanka celebrated like never before. On the streets of Colombo citizens were jubilant. Across the capital the burst of firecrackers that had begun the previous day, intensified as people poured out on the streets, waving Sri Lankan flags, singing patriotic songs, clearly happy that the single biggest fear factor—the LTTE's ability to strike anywhere on the island—was finally eliminated from their lives.

The Sinhalas were understandably aggressive but surprisingly, even Tamils in their strongholds like Wellawath were relieved that the LTTE was eliminated.

As a young Tamil boy told me in a middle of a procession: "Now we Tamils will at least not be perpetual suspects in the eyes of the Army and the police."

But that was perhaps just for record.

Deep down, the Tamils had mixed feelings.

While most despised Prabhakaran for his despotic and totalitarian methods and for bringing misery to them, many also believed that the LTTEs presence gave the Tamils a semblance of a chance to have a dignified existence in Sri Lanka.

With Prabhkaran gone, they felt, Tamils would remain permanent second class citizens.

President Rajapaksa's biggest challenge would therefore be to win the peace by sparking reconciliation between its majority Sinhalese and minority Tamil ethnic populations, healing a rift that looks unbridgeable.

But Mahinda Rajapaksa is nothing if not shrewd. He knows the importance of symbolism. So during a speech in Parliament to announce the victory in Eelam War IV, he began by speaking a few sentences in Tamil. In that highly symbolic gesture, Rajapaksa called on fellow Sri Lankans to distinguish between the Tamil Tigers and the rest of the Tamil people. With the Tigers gone, he said, "we all must now live as equals in this free country." "Now there is nothing called majority and minority in this country. There are only patriotic and non-patriotic people," he added for good effect.

But the reconciliation is easier wished than achieved. Rajapaksa will have to restore to their homes and livelihoods some 300,000 Tamils in the North, a major chunk of the population of that region, who fled the fighting only to be housed in Internally Displaced People camps.

In fact, how the government handles the IDP issue in the coming months will determine its international image. Described by some UN representatives as internment camps, the camps have continued to draw adverse criticism from international community and International NGOs on various counts of living conditions, health, denial of freedom of movement etc.

During talks with an Indian delegation led by NSA MK Narayanan in the immediate aftermath of the victory, Rajapaksa had given a 180-day deadline to rehabilitate the people back in their original homes. That deadline may not be met.

France, the U.S. and the U.K. have come out with strong statements on the need for restoration of normal life in the war affected areas. The U.S. has also emphasized the need for implementing the 13th Amendment of the Sri Lanka constitution giving limited autonomy to the provincial councils.

The handling of Wanni issues also figured during the visit of Sri Lanka's high-powered delegation to India in July.

However, the President appears to be in no hurry to implement the 13th amendment of the constitution—one of India's pet demands—in full, despite repeated promises to do so after the eastern province election.

He may have a reason to delay the implementation though. Rajapaksa is perhaps getting ready to advance the Presidential election to early 2010 and then implement the 13th amendment after getting a stronger manadate from the people. This will enable the President to do away with the dependence upon other smaller parties like the Leftist Janatha Vimukthi Peramuna (JVP) and the right wing Jathika Hela Urumaya (JHU).

Rajapaksa's biggest challenge, as noted political commentator Rohan Gunaratna said in a recent article, would be to unite the people. "The third task is if anything the hardest: to encourage the people of Sri Lanka—Sinhalese, Tamils, Muslims and Burghers—to think and act "Sri Lankan." Sri Lanka belongs to all its inhabitants. If a minority of the Sinhalese wrongly claims that Sri Lanka belongs to the Sinhalese, then the Tamils will claim the north and Muslims the east. As the majority, the Sinhalese must be more generous to its minorities. Misguided nationalists, both Sinhalese and Tamils, once came close to destroying the country. A lesson is that religion, language and caste should never again be used to build political strength. All Sri Lankans have an obligation to rebuild the broken bridges between the different communities, and resist ethnic and religious entrepreneurs who seek to divide people on the basis of their ethnicity or faith."

Saner elements in the Sri Lankan society are also worried about the increasing militarization of the country. They point out that the government has plans to expand the military massively.

The government is indeed totally revamping the national security setup. With the plans to modernize the navy and expansion of the army to a 300,000 strong force already in place, the creation of the post of CDS (Chief of Defence Staff) and appointment of Gen Fonseka as the first CDS are significant and would be watched with keen interest by neighbors.

The new CDS will have a staff of 300 including seven Major Generals, one Rear Admiral, and an Air Vice Marshal. The staff includes Chief of Staff, a Director General Joint Planning and Defence

Development, Director Joint Intelligence, War Assistant to the CDS, War Secretary to CDS, and Director Research and Development.

Post-war, many formation commanders who did a commendable job during the conflict have been rewarded with diplomatic and key administrative appointments.

The civil society is also worried about the lack of tolerance to criticism by the government. Many journalists and human rights activists remain in exile having fled the country during the conflict and having fallen foul of the government for questioning the conduct of the war.

During the war and in its immediate aftermath however, it was apparent that Sri Lanka was the victim of the West's double standards. Here's a nation that secured a hard-earned military victory over what was unarguably the world's most dreaded and ruthless terrorist group. LTTE was the outfit that gave the world the suicide vest and suicide belt that were responsible for the assassination of at least one President and a former Prime Minister across two nations, this was the group that killed and wounded at least 70,000 people over a quarter century; here was a group who's writ ran large over one-third of a sovereign nation.

And to top it all, the LTTE had kept over 250,000 innocent, hapless Tamil civilians—women, children, the young and the old—hostage for over two years and mercilessly used them as an insurance against the advancing Sri Lankan army.

If ever there was a ripe case for a well-planned and executed military operation, here it was in Sri Lanka.

President Mahinda Rajapaksa and his team went about prosecuting what, by all accounts, was a legitimate war.

But the world, particularly the Western world went into an overdrive to stop Colombo. Norway, Sweden, the UK and to a lesser extent the United States put pressure on Sri Lanka by various means. Some threatened to move a resolution in the UN, others lobbied to prevent a bailout package mooted by the International Monetary Fund for the war-ravaged country.

Now, many have called for war crime investigations into the conduct of the Sri Lankan military. Had it not been for countries like Russia, China and to some extent India, Sri Lanka would have suffered grievously at the hands of the so-called liberal lobby, ably aided and abetted by the 'bleeding-heart' liberals among the western media who think they are the judge, jury and executors when it comes to dealing with Asian and African nations.

All of them had tried to stop the war in Sri Lanka, ostensibly to safeguard the civilians but in reality the efforts were directed at rescuing LTTE chief Vellupillai Prabhakaran and his top associates.

The simple and bitter truth is: the Western world has not been able to digest the fact that a small, underdeveloped nation like Sri Lanka has managed to defeat a terrorist group, a feat that they have not managed despite deploying huge resources and manpower across the globe.

So why is it that a small nation's victory over terrorism "fit to be tried for war crimes," but a big bully's (like the US) blatant violation of human rights is part of a "necessary war on terrorism"?

Why didn't any one of these defenders of human rights put pressure on the LTTE when it was taking hundreds of thousands of civilians along with it as it retreated during the war?

If ever there is a clear case of the western nations' hypocrisy, it is demonstrated here in India's backyard, in Sri Lanka.

Let Washington and London and Bonn and Ottawa first look at their own conduct before trying to prosecute a small country for doing what any sovereign nation has a right to do.

In the wake of the war, friends—military officers and civil servants alike—have often asked me how a powerful terrorist organization like the LTTE was brought down to its knees. As I have said in the preceding pages, the LTTE's decimation can be attributed to two or three big reasons.

One, the Sri Lankan armed forces were given, for the first time in decades, a clear politico-military objective by President Mahinda Rajapaksa: destroy the LTTE militarily. Sri Lanka's Army chief, Gen.

Sarath Fonseka explained, in an interview to me, the difference between earlier military campaigns and this one, in one simple sentence: "This time we were playing for a win, not for a draw."

Second, there was much greater synergy among the three forces. That and opening of multiple fronts against the LTTE coupled with innovative military tactics, led to an impressive military victory.

Third, countries like China, Russia and even India provided strong military and political support.

Fourth, Prabhakaran, who lived and survived on sheer instinct in the past, made the fatal mistake of keeping over 300,000 Tamil civilians with him, as he retreated. These civilians hobbled him severely.

The war may have ended, but the Sri Lankan story is not over yet.

President Rajapaksa and his team must avoid triumphalism to spoil the enormous goodwill that they have earned by winning the war.

They must ensure that the death of one Prabhakaran does not lead to the birth of another.

Therein lies Mahinda Rajapaksa's biggest test.

ANNEXURES

THE FEB 2002 CEASEFIRE AGREEMENT

Agreement on a ceasefire between the Government of the Democratic Socialist Republic of Sri Lanka and the Liberation Tigers of Tamil Eelam

Preamble

The overall objective of the Government of the Democratic Socialist Republic of Sri Lanka (hereinafter referred to as the GOSL) and the Liberation Tigers of Tamil Eelam (hereinafter referred to as the LTTE) is to find a negotiated solution to the ongoing ethnic conflict in Sri Lanka.

The GOSL and the LTTE (hereinafter referred to as the Parties) recognize the importance of bringing an end to the hostilities and improving the living conditions for all inhabitants affected by the conflict. Bringing an end to the hostilities is also seen by the Parties as a means of establishing a positive atmosphere in which further steps towards negotiations on a lasting solution can be taken.

The Parties further recognize that groups that are not directly party to the conflict are also suffering the consequences of it. This is particularly the case as regards the Muslim population. Therefore, the provisions of this Agreement regarding the security of civilians and their property apply to all inhabitants.

With reference to the above, the Parties have agreed to enter into a ceasefire, refrain from conduct that could undermine the good intentions or violate the spirit of this Agreement and implement confidence-building measures as indicated in the articles below.

Article 1: Modalities of a ceasefire

The Parties have agreed to implement a ceasefire between their armed forces as follows:

1.1 A jointly agreed ceasefire between the GOSL and the LTTE shall enter into force on such date as is notified by the Norwegian Minister of Foreign Affairs in accordance with Article 4.2, hereinafter referred to as D-day.

Military operations

1.2 Neither Party shall engage in any offensive military operation. This requires the total cessation of all military action and includes, but is not limited to, such acts as:

(a) The firing of direct and indirect weapons, armed raids, ambushes, assassinations, abductions, destruction of civilian or military property, sabotage, suicide missions and activities by deep penetration units;

(b) Aerial bombardment;

(c) Offensive naval operations.

1.3 The Sri Lankan armed forces shall continue to perform their legitimate task of safeguarding the sovereignty and territorial integrity of Sri Lanka without engaging in offensive operations against the LTTE.

Separation of forces

1.4 Where forward defence localities have been established, the GOSL's armed forces and the LTTE's fighting formations shall hold their ground positions, maintaining a zone of separation of a minimum of six hundred (600) metres. However, each Party reserves the right of movement within one hundred (100) metres of its own defence localities, keeping an absolute minimum distance of four hundred (400) metres between them. Where existing positions are closer than four hundred (400) metres, no such right of movement applies and the Parties agree to ensure the maximum possible distance between their personnel.

1.5 In areas where localities have not been clearly established, the status quo as regards the areas controlled by the GOSL and the LTTE, respectively, on 24 December 2001 shall continue to apply pending such demarcation as is provided in article 1.6.

1.6 The Parties shall provide information to the Sri Lanka Monitoring Mission (SLMM) regarding defence localities in all areas of contention, cf. Article 3. The monitoring mission shall assist the Parties in drawing up demarcation lines at the latest by D-day + 30.

1.7 The Parties shall not move munitions, explosives or military equipment into the area controlled by the other Party.

1.8 Tamil paramilitary groups shall be disarmed by the GOSL by D-day + 30 at the latest. The GOSL shall offer to integrate individuals in these units under the command and disciplinary structure of the GOSL armed forces for service away from the Northern and Eastern Province.

Freedom of movement

1.9 The Parties' forces shall initially stay in the areas under their respective control, as provided in Article 1.4 and Article 1.5.

1.10 Unarmed GOSL troops shall, as of D- day + 60, be permitted unlimited passage between Jaffna and Vavunyia using the Jaffna-Kandy road (A9). The modalities are to be worked out by the Parties with the assistance of the SLMM.

1.11 The Parties agree that as of D-day individual combatants shall, on the recommendation of their area commander, be permitted, unarmed and in plain clothes, to visit family and friends residing in areas under the control of the other Party. Such visits shall be limited to six days every second month, not including the time of travel by the shortest applicable route. The LTTE shall facilitate the use of the Jaffna-Kandy road for this purpose. The Parties reserve the right to deny entry to specified military areas.

1.12 The Parties agree that as of D-day individual combatants shall, notwithstanding the two-month restriction, be permitted, unarmed and in plain clothes, to visit immediate family (i.e.

spouses, children, grandparents, parents and siblings) in connection with weddings or funerals. The right to deny entry to specified military areas applies.

1.13 Fifty (50) unarmed LTTE members shall as of D-day + 30, for the purpose of political work, be permitted freedom of movement in the areas of the North and the East dominated by the GOSL. Additional 100 unarmed LTTE members shall be permitted freedom of movement as of D-day + 60. As of D-day + 90, all unarmed LTTE members shall be permitted freedom of movement in the North and the East. The LTTE members shall carry identity papers. The right of the GOSL to deny entry to specified military areas applies.

Article 2: Measures to restore normalcy

The Parties shall undertake the following confidence-building measures with the aim of restoring normalcy for *all* inhabitants of Sri Lanka:

2.1 The Parties shall in accordance with international law abstain from hostile acts against the civilian population, including such acts as torture, intimidation, abduction, extortion and harassment.

2.2 The Parties shall refrain from engaging in activities or propagating ideas that could offend cultural or religious sensitivities. Places of worship (temples, churches, mosques and other holy sites, etc.) currently held by the forces of either of the Parties shall be vacated by D-day + 30 and made accessible to the public. Places of worship which are situated in "high security zones" shall be vacated by all armed personnel and maintained in good order by civilian workers, even when they are not made accessible to the public.

2.3 Beginning on the date on which this Agreement enters into force, school buildings occupied by either Party shall be vacated and returned to their intended use. This activity shall be completed by D-day + 160 at the latest.

2.4 A schedule indicating the return of all other public buildings to their intended use shall be drawn up by the Parties and published at the latest by D-day + 30.

2.5 The Parties shall review the security measures and the set-up of checkpoints, particularly in densely populated cities and towns, in order to introduce systems that will prevent harassment of the civilian population. Such systems shall be in place from D-day + 60.

2.6 The Parties agree to ensure the unimpeded flow of non-military goods to and from the LTTE-dominated areas with the exception of certain items as shown in Annex A. Quantities shall be determined by market demand. The GOSL shall regularly review the matter with the aim of gradually removing any remaining restrictions on non-military goods.

2.7 In order to facilitate the flow of goods and the movement of civilians, the Parties agree to establish checkpoints on their line of control at such locations as are specified in Annex B.

2.8 The Parties shall take steps to ensure that the Trincomalee-Habarana road remains open on a 24-hour basis for passenger traffic with effect from D-day + 10.

2.9 The Parties shall facilitate the extension of the rail service on the Batticaloa-line to Welikanda. Repairs and maintenance shall be carried out by the GOSL in order to extend the service up to Batticaloa.

2.10 The Parties shall open the Kandy-Jaffna road (A9) to non-military traffic of goods and passengers. Specific modalities shall be worked out by the Parties with the assistance of the Royal Norwegian Government by D-day + 30 at the latest.

2.11 A gradual easing of the fishing restrictions shall take place starting from D-day. As of D-day + 90, all restrictions on day and night fishing shall be removed, subject to the following exceptions: (i) fishing will not be permitted on (hereinafter referred to as the SLMM).

2.12 The Parties agree that search operations and arrests under the Prevention of Terrorism Act shall not take place. Arrests shall be conducted under due process of law in accordance with the Criminal Procedure Code.

2.13 The Parties agree to provide family members of detainees access to the detainees within D-day + 30.

Article 3: The Sri Lanka Monitoring Mission

The Parties have agreed to set up an international monitoring mission to enquire into any instance of violation of the terms and conditions of this Agreement. Both Parties shall fully cooperate to rectify any matter of conflict caused by their respective sides. The mission shall conduct international verification through on-site monitoring of the fulfilment of the commitments entered into in this Agreement as follows:

3.1 The name of the monitoring mission shall be the Sri Lanka Monitoring Mission

3.2 Subject to acceptance by the Parties, the Royal Norwegian Government (hereinafter referred to as the RNG) shall appoint the Head of the SLMM (hereinafter referred to as the HoM), who shall be the final authority regarding interpretation of this Agreement.

3.3 The SLMM shall liaise with the Parties and report to the RNG.

3.4 The HoM shall decide the date for the commencement of the SLMM's operations.

3.5 The SLMM shall be composed of representatives from Nordic countries.

3.6 The SLMM shall establish a headquarters in such place as the HoM finds appropriate. An office shall be established in Colombo and in Vanni in order to liaise with the GOSL and the LTTE, respectively. The SLMM will maintain a presence in the districts of Jaffna, Mannar, Vavuniya, Trincomalee, Batticaloa and Amparai.within an area of 1 nautical mile on either side along the coast and 2 nautical miles seawards from all security forces camps on the coast; (ii) fishing will not be permitted in harbours or approaches to harbours, bays and estuaries along the coast.

3.7 A local monitoring committee shall be established in Jaffna, Mannar, Vavuniya, Trincomalee, Batticaloa and Amparai. Each committee shall consist of five members, two appointed by the GOSL, two by the LTTE and one international monitor appointed by the HoM. The international monitor shall chair the committee. The GOSL and the LTTE appointees may be selected from among retired judges, public servants, religious leaders or similar leading citizens.

3.8 The committees shall serve the SLMM in an advisory capacity and discuss issues relating to the implementation of this Agreement in their respective districts, with a view to establishing a common understanding of such issues. In particular, they will seek to resolve any dispute concerning the implementation of this Agreement at the lowest possible level.

3.9 The Parties shall be responsible for the appropriate protection of and security arrangements for all SLMM members.

3.10 The Parties agree to ensure the freedom of movement of the SLMM members in performing their tasks. The members of the SLMM shall be given immediate access to areas where violations of the Agreement are alleged to have taken place. The Parties also agree to facilitate the widest possible access to such areas for the local members of the six above-mentioned committees, cf. Article 3.7.

3.11 It shall be the responsibility of the SLMM to take immediate action on any complaints made by either Party to the Agreement, and to enquire into and assist the Parties in the settlement of any dispute that might arise in connection with such complaints.

3.12 With the aim of resolving disputes at the lowest possible level, communication shall be established between commanders of the GOSL armed forces and the LTTE area leaders to enable them to resolve problems in the conflict zones.

3.13 Guidelines for the operations of the SLMM shall be established in a separate document.

Article 4: Entry into force, amendments and termination of the Agreement

4.1 Each Party shall notify its consent to be bound by this Agreement through a letter to the Norwegian Minister of Foreign Affairs signed by Prime Minister Ranil Wickremesinghe on behalf of the GOSL and by leader Velupillai Pirabaharan on behalf of the LTTE, respectively. The Agreement shall be initialled by each Party and enclosed in the above-mentioned letter.

4.2 The Agreement shall enter into force on such date as is notified by the Norwegian Minister of Foreign Affairs.

4.3 This Agreement may be amended and modified by mutual agreement of both Parties. Such amendments shall be notified in writing to the RNG.

4.4 This Agreement shall remain in force until notice of termination is given by either Party to the RNG. Such notice shall be given fourteen (14) days in advance of the effective date of termination.

ANNEXURE A

The Parties agree to ensure the flow of non-military goods to and from LTTE dominated areas of the Northern and Eastern Province, as well as unimpeded flow of such goods to the civilian population in these areas. Non military goods not covered by article 2.6 in the Agreement are listed below:

- Non military arms/ammunition
- Explosives
- Remote control devices
- Barbed wire
- Binoculars/Telescopes
- Compasses
- Penlight batteries

Diesel, petrol, cement and iron rods will be restricted in accordance with the following procedures and quantities:

Diesel and petrol

The Government Agents (GA) will register available vehicles; tractors and motorcycles in the LTTE controlled areas. The GA will calculate the required weekly amount of diesel and petrol based on the following estimate:

Trucks/Buses	250 litre/week
4 wheels tractor	310 litre/week
2 wheel tractor	40 litre/week
Petrol vehicle	30 litre/week
Motorcycles	7 litre/week
Fishing vessels	400 litre/week

Cement

Cement required for rehabilitation and reconstruction of Government property; registeret co-operatives; or approved housing projects implemented by the GOSL and international NGOs and more affluent members of the society; will be brought in directly by relevant institutions under licenses issued by Government Agents. The GA shall stipulate the monthly quantities permitted for such project based upon planned and reported progress.

Cement required for individual shops/constructions/house owners/rehabilitation-initiatives will be made available through the co-operations on a commercial basis. The monthly import for this purpose wil be limited to 5000 bags during the first month and thereafter 10 000 bags/month. Individual sales by the co-operatives will be registered and limited to 25 bags per household.

Iron rods

Iron rods for building constructions will be brought in to the LTTE controlled areas under licenses issued by the GA.

A monthly reassessment will be made to assess the possibilites of removal of the above restrictions.

ANNEXURE B

Checkpoints agreed in ¤ 2.7 are as follows:

- Mandur
- Paddirupur
- Kaludaveli Ferry Point
- Anbalantivu Ferry Point
- Mamunai Ferry Point
- Vanvunateevu
- Santhiveli Boat Point
- Black Bridge
- Sitandy Boat Point
- Kiran bridge
- Kinniyadi Boat Point
- Valachenai
- Makerni
- Mahindapura
- Muttur
- Ugilankulam
- Oma

Posted by USIP Library on: February 25, 2002 and March 18, 2002.

Source Name: Web site of the Norwegian Ministry of Foreign Affairs for text of the agreement.

Source Name: Embassy of Norway in Washington, D.C. for text of Annexes A and B via e-mail.

Source URL:

http://www.odin.dep.no/ud/norsk/aktuelt/pressem/032171-290002/index-dok000-b-n-a.html

Date downloaded: February 22, 2002.

Date e-mailed: March 13 2002

Note: Paragraphs 3.2 through 3.6 have been moved from their position in the text on the web site to follow the numerical sequence. Text of Annexes A and B are inserted at the end of the agreement.

THE INDO-SRI LANKA ACCORD

To establish peace and normalcy in Sri Lanka the president of the Democratic Socialist Republic of Sri Lanka, his Excellency Mr. J.R. Jayawardene, and the Prime Minister of The Republic of India, His Excellency Mr. Rajiv Gandhi, having met at Colombo on July 29, 1987.

Attaching utmost importance to nurturing, intensifying and strengthening the traditional friendship of Sri Lanka and India, and acknowledging the imperative need of resolving the ethnic problem of Sri Lanka, and the consequent violence, and for the safety, wellbeing and prosperity of people belonging to all communities of Sri Lanka,

Have this day entered into the following agreement to fulfil this Objective.

In this context,

1.1 desiring to preserve the unity, sovereignty and territorial integrity of Sri Lanka,

1.2 acknowledging that Sri Lanka is a "multi-ethnic and multi-lingual plural society" consisting, *inter-alia*, of Sinhalese, Tamils, Muslims (Moors) and Burgers,

1.3 recognising that each ethnic group has a distinct cultural and linguistic identity, which has to be carefully nurtured,

1.4 Also recognising that the northern and the eastern provinces have been areas of historical habitation of Sri Lankan Tamil speaking peoples, who have at all times hitherto lived together in this territory with other ethnic groups,

1.5 conscious of the necessity of strengthening the forces contributing to the unity, sovereignty and territorial integrity of Sri Lanka, and preserving its character as a multi-ethnic, multi-lingual and multi- religious plural society in which all citizens can live in equality, safety and harmony, and prosper and fulfil their aspirations,

2. RESOLVE THAT

2.1 Since the Government of Sri Lanka proposes to permit adjoining provinces to join to form one administrative unit and also by a referendum to separate as may be permitted to the northern and eastern provinces as outlined below:

2.2 During the period, which shall be considered an interim period (i.e. from the date of the elections to the provincial council, as specified in para 2.8 to the date of the referendum as specified in para 2.3), the northern and eastern provinces as now constituted, will form one administrative unit, having one elected provincial council. Such a unit will have one governor, one chief minister and one board of ministers.

2.3 There will be a referendum on or before 31st December 1988 to enable the people of the eastern province to decide whether:

(a) The eastern province should remain linked with the northern province as one administrative unit, and continue to be governed together with the northern province as specified in para 2.2 or:

(b) The eastern province should constitute a separate administrative unit having its own distinct provincial council with a separate governor, chief minister and board of ministers. The president may, at his discretion, decide to postpone such a referendum.

2.4 All persons, who have been displaced due to ethnic violence or other reasons, will have the right to vote in such a referendum. Necessary conditions to enable them to return to areas from where they were displaced will be created.

2.5 The referendum, when held, will be monitored by a committee headed by the chief Justice, a member appointed by the President, nominated by the government of Sri Lanka, and a member appointed by the president, nominated by the representatives of the Tamil speaking people of the eastern province.

2.6 A simple majority will be sufficient to determine the result of the referendum.

2.7 Meetings and other forms of propaganda, permissible within the laws of the country, will be allowed before the referendum.

2.8 Elections to provincial councils will be held within the next three months, in any event before 31st December 1987. Indian observers will be invited for elections to the provincial council of the north and east.

2.9 The emergency will be lifted in the eastern and northern provinces by Aug. 15, 1987. A cessation of hostilities will come into effect all over the island within 48 hours of signing of this agreement. All arms presently held by militant groups will be surrendered in accordance with an agreed procedure to authorities to be designated by the government of Sri Lanka.

Consequent to the cessation of hostilities and the surrender of arms by militant groups, the army and other security personnel will be confined to barracks in camps as on 25 May 1987. The process of surrendering arms and the confining of security personnel moving back to barracks shall be completed within 72 hours of the cessation of hostilities coming into effect.

2.10 The government of Sri Lanka will utilise for the purpose of law enforcement and maintenance of security in the northern and eastern provinces same organisations and mechanisms of government as are used in the rest of the country.

2.11 The President of Sri Lanka will grant a general amnesty to political and other prisoners now held in custody under The Prevention of Terrorism Act and other emergency laws, and to combatants, as well as to those persons accused, charged and/or convicted under these laws. The Government of Sri Lanka will make special efforts to rehabilitate militant youth with a view to bringing them back into the mainstream of national life. India will co-operate in the process.

2.12 The government of Sri Lanka will accept and abide by the above provisions and expect all others to do likewise.

2.13 If the framework for the resolutions is accepted, the Government of Sri Lanka will implement the relevant proposals forthwith.

2.14 The government of India will underwrite and guarantee the resolutions, and co-operate in the implementation of these proposals.

2.15 These proposals are conditional to an acceptance of the proposals negotiated from 4.5.1986 to 19.12.1986. Residual matters not finalised during the above negotiations shall be resolved between India and Sri Lanka within a period of six weeks of signing this agreement. These proposals are also conditional to the Government of India co-operating directly with the Government of Sri Lanka in their implementation.

2.16 These proposals are also conditional to the Government of India taking the following actions if any militant groups operating in Sri Lanka do not accept this framework of proposals for a settlement, namely,

(a) India will take all necessary steps to ensure that Indian Territory is not used for activities prejudicial to the unity, integrity and security of Sri Lanka

(b) The Indian navy/coast guard will cooperate with the Sri Lankan navy in preventing Tamil militant activities from affecting Sri Lanka.

(c) In the event that the Government of Sri Lanka requests the Government of India to afford military assistance to implement these proposals the Government of India will co-operate by giving to the Government of Sri Lanka such military assistance as and when requested.

(d) The Government of India will expedite repatriation from Sri Lanka of Indian citizens to India who are resident here, concurrently with the repatriation of Sri Lankan refugees from Tamil Nadu.

(e) The Governments of Sri Lanka and India will co-operate in ensuring the physical security and safety of all communities inhabiting the northern and eastern provinces.

2.17 The government of Sri Lanka shall ensure free, full and fair participation of voters from all communities in the northern and eastern provinces in electoral processes envisaged in this agreement. The government of India will extend full co-operation to the government of Sri Lanka in this regard.

2.18 The official language of Sri Lanka shall be Sinhala. Tamil and English will also be official languages.

3. This agreement and the Annexure thereto shall come into force upon signature.

In witness whereof, we have set our hands and seals hereunto.

Done in Colombo, Sri Lanka, on this the twenty-ninth day of July of the year one thousand nine hundred and eighty seven, in duplicate, both texts being equally authentic.

Junius Richard Jayawardene
President of the Democratic of the Socialist Republic of Sri Lanka

Rajiv Gandhi
Prime Minister Republic of India

ANNEXURE TO THE AGREEMENT

1. His Excellency the President of Sri Lanka and the Prime Minister of India agree that the referendum mentioned in paragraph 2 and its sub-paragraphs of the agreement will be observed by a representative of the election Commission of India to be invited by His Excellency the President of Sri Lanka.

2. Similarly, both heads of Government agree that the elections to the provincial council mentioned in paragraph 2.8 of the agreement will be observed and all para-military personnel will be withdrawn from the eastern and northern provinces with a view to creating conditions conducive to fair elections to the council.

3. The President, in his discretion shall absorb such para-military forces, which came into being due to ethnic violence, into the regular security forces of Sri Lanka.

4. The President of Sri Lanka and the Prime Minister of India agree that the Tamil militants shall surrender their arms to authorities agreed upon to be designated by the President of Sri Lanka. The surrender shall take place in the presence of one senior representative each of the Sri Lanka Red Cross and the Indian Red Cross.

5. The President of Sri Lanka and the Prime Minister of India agree that a joint Indo-Sri Lankan observer group consisting of qualified representatives of the Government of Sri Lanka and the Government of India would monitor the cessation of hostilities from 31 July 1987.

6. The President of Sri Lanka and the Prime Minister of India also agree that in the terms of paragraph 2.14 and paragraph 2.16(c) of the agreement, an Indian peace keeping contingent may be invited by the President of Sri Lanka to guarantee and enforce the cessation of hostilities, if so required.

EXCHANGE OF LETTERS BETWEEN THE PRIME MINISTER OF INDIA AND THE PRESIDENT OF SRI LANKA.

Excellency,

1. Conscious of the friendship between our two countries stretching over two millenia and more, and recognizing the importance of nurturing this traditional friendship, it is imperative that both Sri Lanka and India reaffirm the decision not to allow our respective territories to be used for activities prejudicial to each other's unity, territorial integrity and security.

2. In this spirit, you had, in the course of our discussions agreed to meet some of India's concerns as follows:

(i) Your Excellency and myself will reach an early understanding about the relevance and employment of foreign military and intelligence personnel with a view to ensuring that such presences will not prejudice Indo-Sri Lankan relations.

(ii) Trincomalee or any other ports in Sri Lanka will not be made available for military use by any country in a manner prejudicial to India's interests.

(iii) The work of resotoring and operating the Trincomalee Oil Tank Farm will be undertaken as a joint venture between India and Sri Lanka.

(iv) Sri Lanka's agreements with foreign broadcasting organizations will be reviewed to ensure that any facilities set up by them in Sri Lanka.

3. In the same spirit India will:

(i) deport all Sri Lankan citizens who are found to be engaging in terrorist activities or advocating separatism or secessionism.

(ii) provide training facilities and military supplies for Sri Lankan forces.

4. India and Sri Lanka have agreed to set up a joint consultative mechanism to continuously review matters of common concern in the light of the objectives stated in paragraph 1 and specifically to monitor the implementation of other matters contained in this letter.

5. Kindly confirm, Excellency, that the above correctly sets out the agreement reached between us.

Please accept, Excellency, the assurances of my highest consideration.

Yours sincerely,
Rajiv Gandhi

INDEX

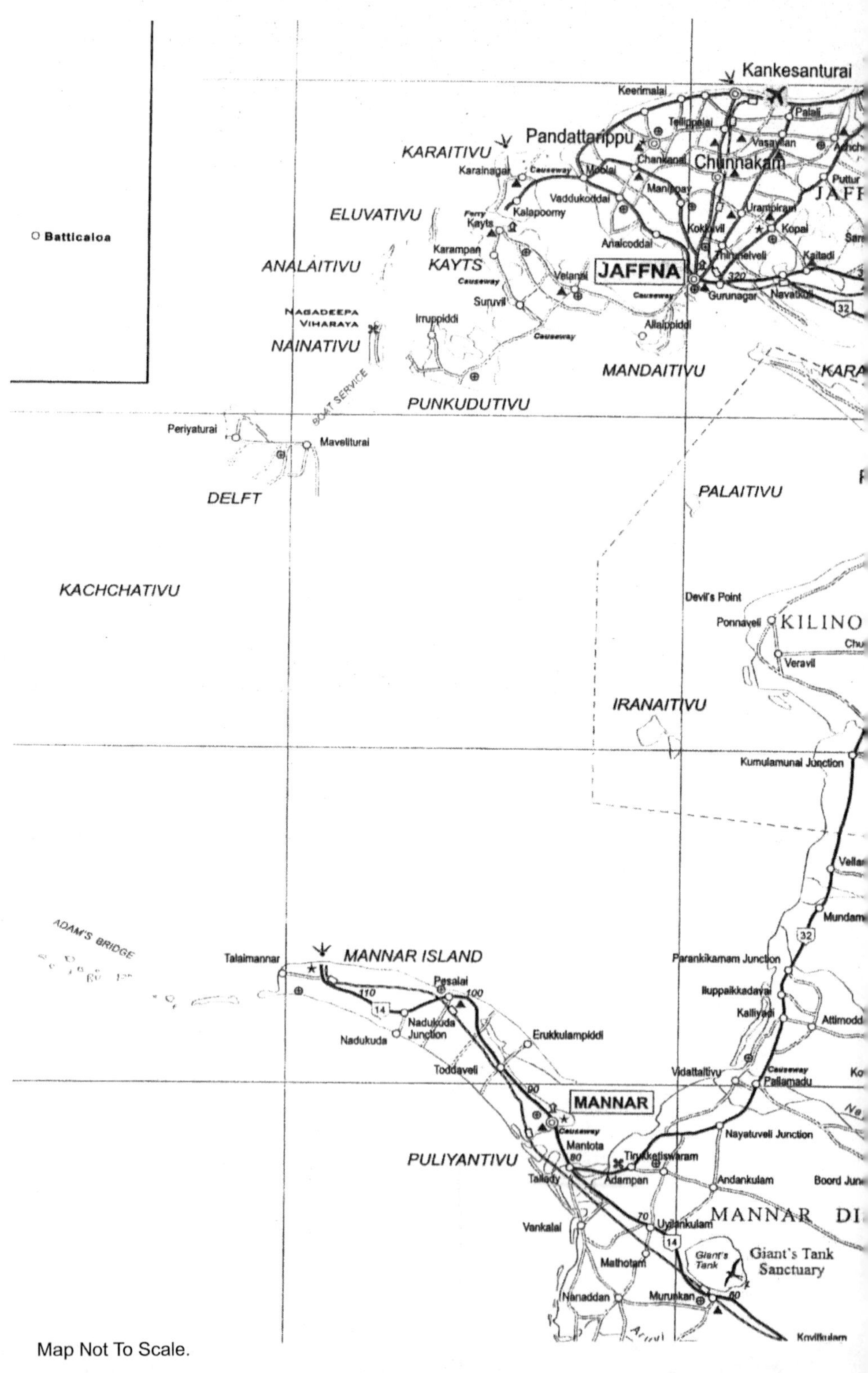

Map Not To Scale.